Dear
Ravi,
may this boo[...]
you an abundance [...]
Love & Light, Alexandra

MW01601375

Dear Ravi,
may this book bring
you an abundance of
Love & Light. Alexandra

THE *Beauty* OF *Wings*

A True Story of Transformation from Near Death to Unconditional Love

ALEXANDRA MIKA

BALBOA PRESS
A DIVISION OF HAY HOUSE

Balboa Press books may be ordered through booksellers or by contacting:

Balboa Press
A Division of Hay House
1663 Liberty Drive
Bloomington, IN 47403
www.balboapress.com
1 (877) 407-4847

Print information available on the last page.

ISBN: 978-1-5043-2942-2 (sc)
ISBN: 978-1-5043-2944-6 (hc)
ISBN: 978-1-5043-2943-9 (e)

Library of Congress Control Number: 2015904132

Balboa Press rev. date: 04/28/2015

This book is dedicated to Mother Earth.

Contents

Chapter 1: The Heat of Transformation 1
Chapter 2: Trials and Tribulations 11
Chapter 3: The Magic of Snowflakes 19
Chapter 4: Close to My Heart 29
Chapter 5: The Beauty of a Broken Wing 39
Chapter 6: The Magnificence of a Pure Inner Being 45
Chapter 7: Free Falling 57
Chapter 8: Silver Wings 81
Chapter 9: Butterflies, Dragonflies, and Bees 87
Chapter 10: Bliss 93
Chapter 11: A Broken Bone, an Alive Wound, and a Hopeful Spirit 101
Chapter 12: The Beauty of Muscles 109

As I feel the intense heat of change, transformation, and growth within my inner workings, the land reminds me of my greater purpose and the greater whole. As I watch the summer flowers wither away and the birds flying south, I am reminded of my own rhythms and I start to remember why I am here.

CHAPTER 1

The Heat of Transformation

August 12, 2009
Dear Diary,

A beautiful pink butterfly began to emerge from my heart during a deep meditation. She was exquisitely detailed and radiant with massive pink and silver iridescent wings. Her thick feet were strong and grounded, and her green eyes glowed with deep strength. She came to me for a specific purpose.

One Month Later

A small orange butterfly landed on my running shoe while I was stretching in preparation for a ten-mile trail run. The butterfly's feet were small enough to coil tightly around a single shoelace, and her beautiful orange wings fluttered in the wind. As she took off from my shoe, another butterfly appeared. The two butterflies began to dance together. They circled each other, flew up and down together, and landed on the same flower simultaneously. As I watched them flirt, I fantasized about true love; an unconditional love that was deeper than flesh and bones.

After this mesmerizing encounter with the butterflies, I headed up the mountain trail in Ashland, Oregon's Tolman Creek Park. The dusty trail and the sound of my pink running shorts flapping in the wind brought a smile to my face. As I ran past the towering forest of trees, I thought about my mother. She was coming to visit soon. My mother had come from Minnesota every few months since I moved to Oregon to attend Lewis and Clark College and then the University of Portland for nursing school. Each visit from my mother felt like a first. Anticipation and excitement always preceded her arrival. My mother always showed up when I needed her most, and that September stay was nothing short of an extraordinary blessing, a visit neither of us will forget. That visit was divinely orchestrated for a purpose greater than both of us.

My mother arrived at the Medford airport at 5:30 p.m. on September 2, 2009. I had called her earlier that day informing her that I would not be able to pick her up from the airport because I had become ill. I had left work early and was lying in bed with a burning sore throat, fever, and fatigue so severe that I felt my body was made of lead. In my eight years of living in Oregon, I was always able to pick my mother up from the airport; that Wednesday evening was highly unusual for both of us. My mother instead took a taxi to my country cottage in Ashland. As she arrived, I was drifting in and out of alertness. The sound of her knocking on my door and the cows mooing outside woke me from my daze. As I stood up from bed to greet her, I felt very dizzy. I waited for the dizziness to subside and slowly walked towards the door. As I opened the door, my mother was thrilled to see me. She walked in, gave me a hug, and asked how I was doing. I told her how ill I was feeling, and she agreed that I looked unusually tired. After she unloaded her belongings, she spoke in depth about my home; the beautiful rafters on the ceiling, the gorgeous windows, and the breathtaking landscape surrounding it. I lay in bed too tired to stand.

After settling in, she helped herself to a glass of water and sat next to me. Assuming my sore throat and fever would be gone by morning, I told my mother, "I think I will be able to go for a run in the morning and then we can go to our favorite restaurant in town, Morning Glory." Little did we both know that this was the beginning of a journey of a lifetime. The day my mother arrived was the day I started the inward journey of going into a dark cocoon to prepare for a butterfly emergence.

The next morning I awoke to birds chirping outside my window, my mother lying to my right, and an unwanted, persistent sore throat. I knew I would not be able to enjoy an early morning run through the forested trails, which meant I was truly ill. During the previous ten years, I spent the majority of my free moments running through beautiful pastures, mystical landscapes, snow-covered mountain peaks, and alongside glistening streams. My adventurous side loved climbing to new heights, soaring through the wind, and discovering secret trails. Every morning I would put on my old t-shirt, pink running shorts, and dirt-covered running shoes, and head for the trails. As soon as my feet hit the raw earth, my heart would thump with excitement. I used my long legs to carry me up steep mountain trails where I would see breathtaking views of the sun rising across mountains in the distance. The routine of running each morning brought me to a heightened state of joy. Being surrounded by enormous green trees, viewing deer off in the distance, climbing to heights where I felt close to the clouds and near the soaring birds, feeling wind across my cheeks, sweating from my core, feeling my muscles working with each heartbeat, moving my body to the sound of rustling leaves – the combination of all the elements of this experience brought me to a blissful state where I felt powerful and limitless. While running through green pastures I felt as though I was flying like the birds. I felt safe and accepted on the dirt trails among the animals and forest. It brought me to another world, a world of imagination, vivid colors, earth tones, wild animals, mystical trees, and beautiful views. I loved running on the trails, and I knew them from the core of my heart.

It was Thursday, September 3, 2009 at 9:00 a.m., and I was in need of medical attention. I felt weak, dizzy, and dehydrated. While lying in bed I drank as much water as I could choke down. My mother convinced me we needed to go into the urgent care center. I was always reluctant to seek help, a trait I inherited from my father – an attitude of independence and self-reliance. I was not sure I was going to be able to make it to the urgent care center that morning when, upon standing, I felt like I was going to faint. We decided to take it one step at a time. First, my mother helped me get dressed while I was still lying in bed. We then tried to make it to my car. My mother wrapped her hands around my waist and we stumbled across the dirt path through the vine-covered gate to my silver Camry parked on a gravel road. My mother opened the door, lowered down the passenger seat, and then helped me in. I lay down with one hand on my chest and one hand on my stomach, and I prayed to my angels. As my mother was not familiar with the area, I gave her directions and we made it to the doctor within an hour, slowed by road construction along the way. As we entered the urgent care center, I sat down and my mother spoke to the front desk attendant to see if I was able to be seen quickly. My mother's anxiety was heightened, urgency seeping through her words. Any time I was sick she did everything in her power to make me well. As a young child I was very asthmatic; my mother took me to the best asthma specialists in town. Her love for me was expressed in the best way she knew how. She tried to protect me from illness and sadness with her hovering nature. I felt restricted.

Within minutes the nurse called out for me. My mother and I walked back with her. She took my vital signs and discovered that I had low blood pressure, a high heart rate, and a temperature. We were then escorted to another room where we waited patiently for the doctor. After several minutes the doctor walked in and asked how I was doing. I explained to him how sick I was feeling. He listened to my heartbeat, lungs, and stomach, and then told me he thought I had the stomach flu and needed some IV fluids. I agreed to receive the fluids. Then, a nurse came in to start the IV. As a registered nurse I was not afraid of needles. Within minutes the fluids were dripping into my bloodstream. After the whole bag of fluids worked its way into my body, the doctor came back and told me to get some rest. He instructed me to drink a lot of water and said I would be better in a few days.

That night my fever progressed, I awoke to severe sharp pains in my left side, and I sweated profusely. By morning the sheets were drenched. My mother did laundry all morning, hung the sheets out in the sunshine to dry and fed me vegetables, vitamin C, and healing spices. However, that night was worse; I experienced more high fever, more sweats, and sharp pains on my left side. Days inched by, filled with more vitamin C, more laundry, more sheets drying in the sun, and more trips to the grocery store. My adventurous nature felt trapped, constrained, and dampened.

The next day my mother suggested we take a walk through Lithia Park so I could receive some quality sunshine. We drove to the park and strolled through the wooded covered trails next to the glistening blue river which came down from Mt. Ashland. The sunshine against my skin felt warm and soothing. The sound of the river was reassuring, and it felt good to be walking in nature. It was a park I loved and cherished; it was beautiful and magical. After walking several miles I told my mother that I needed to sit down. The left-sided pain had been worsening throughout the morning and for a moment it became very intense. I rested on a bench, hunched over holding my left side. I sat quietly in severe pain and prayed to my angels for help. Without feeling any improvement in the pain, I told my mom to call an ambulance. I told her the pain was so severe I could not move. After five excruciatingly long minutes, we both agreed she would drive me back to the urgent care center.

This time after listening to my lungs, the doctor took a chest x-ray. After reviewing the x-ray, he diagnosed me with left lower lobe pneumonia. I was devastated and in shock; as a nurse I knew how severe pneumonia could be. He prescribed antibiotics and pain medication and told me to follow up in one week.

A week passed. My mother returned home to Minnesota, and I was feeling stronger. I had not yet coughed up mucous or phlegm from the pneumonia, which was highly unusual, but my fever was gone, and the pain had diminished. I was ready to return to work and to my active lifestyle. During a follow-up visit, the doctor took another chest x-ray. He told me I was doing great and could return to work. I asked the doctor when I could run again. He told me I could run the next day. My heart pounded with excitement. I felt relieved that I did not have to wait days or weeks to run again. I was excited to return to my running routine. After growing up in an externally focused culture and becoming an athlete, my body had become my identity; it was my shell. Little did I know that my shell had begun to break wide open.

After visiting with the doctor, I went home to rest. The next morning, I woke up, put on my old t-shirt and pink running shorts, and tied my dirt-covered running shoes, then headed straight to the trails. I always had a strong drive to maintain my endurance, slim physique, and athletic abilities. That morning I jogged up a steep dirt trail winding through thick forested trees. About one mile uphill, I reached an overlook where I could see the sun rising and mountains in the distance. I continued along the trail, passing a beautiful deer off in the woods, two squirrels, and several huge birds flying above me. I felt at home. At about three miles into the run I felt very short of breath and winded, so I returned home and lay down. My left-sided pain came back even more severely than before and my right lung began to hurt. My childhood asthma had returned with full force.

After about one hour of severe pain and discomfort, I went back to the doctor who gave me a nebulizer treatment which did not help. He recommended I return home to rest. The medication in the nebulizer treatment made me jittery. I drove home, even though my hands were shaking. Once home I tried to rest, but was edgy from the nebulizer treatment and anxious about my lungs; resting was not easy. The pain was sharp and severe, so I called the doctor. His advice was to allow my lungs time to heal. I lay in bed anxiously gasping for air. Nothing helped – inhalers, medications, teas, spices, remedies, herbs, and vitamin C were all useless. My world had begun to shatter as my lung capacity shriveled to that of a mouse. I spent the next two weeks in bed short of breath, filled with emotional and physical pain, crying, praying, and distressed about my state of health.

After years of running through snow-covered mountains, mystical forests, and on thrilling trails, lying in bed with minimal air intake and severe pain was heart wrenching. It felt like a fire was smoldering inside me and I could not soothe it. I was in the midst of a heated transformation. My lungs were inflamed and filled with phlegm, and unconditional love was the instrument I needed to stitch my life back together. Patience was vital. Day after day went by; setbacks, shortness of breath, wheezing, and pains were common themes of my daily life that year. As fire consumed the Oregon valley floor that fall, inflammation filled my lungs.

Every morning I spent time meditating next to a burning candle. I spent quiet time feeling my inner world. I began to feel deep sensations within my heart-space. It felt like my heart was beginning to open as a butterfly emerges from a cocoon. I was in the process of awakening to my soul and unconditional love within my heart. Often I would use my third eye (my inner eye) to see the pink, beautiful, enormous butterfly emerging from my heart-space. During my meditations, I set intentions for full healing, full recovery, abundance, happiness, and well-being. I spent time writing in my journal and reading inspirational quotes, one of my favorites said by Helen Keller: "we can do anything we want if we stick to it long enough." Often I would watch the trees sway in the wind and wonder if I would ever be able to run again. I was learning how to be still and tap into the spiritual world.

The quiet time gave me an opportunity to reflect on my childhood. As a sensitive child I was in tune with nature and animals. The trails and creatures understood me, and I in turn understood them. I spent most of my time developing a deep relationship with the natural world and animals. The trees gave me strength, the animals spoke to my heart, and the trails brought out my adventurous spirit. I felt safe in nature and with animals, especially horses. I rode horses daily as a child and teen. The horses and nature were my source of unconditional love.

I was teased and tormented in school, during sports, at the horseback riding stable, and at home; as a result, I turned towards nature and horses for comfort and safety. I grew unusually fast and by the sixth grade I measured six feet tall. In junior high I was teased daily for being a gross giant, too big and too tall. I was laughed at, ridiculed, excluded, and called "ostrich legs." I was shunned everywhere I went. At home my older brother tormented me. He threw things at me, shoved me into dark spaces, and told me I was too ugly to ever have a boyfriend. My father was emotionally absent or loud with anger, and my mother was highly judgmental. I was a very asthmatic child.

As a result, I developed a very poor body image, seeing myself as a "gross giant." I felt like the ugly duckling who no one would ever love. I wanted to be small and petite. I did not feel safe around humans nor did I trust them, but I did trust nature and animals. My free time was spent with the horses and in the outdoors. I began running in high school which became a physical release for me. By college I was dieting and running obsessively, still struggling with a very poor body image. My world felt broken when I became ill and was not able to run on the trails and commune with nature in the way I was accustomed. My safe haven and emotional release was gone. A new way of being was emerging within me, and the future years would reveal my true essence.

As I let go of strings, cords, and heavy rocks, I expand my wings even more and start to feel the ground beneath my feet, the air against my cheek and the heat of the sun. As I allow my inner spark to warm my body with radiant light, I shed what is no longer needed and I step clearly into my light.

CHAPTER 2

Trials and Tribulations

That October tested me in ways I had never been tested before, and I have since come to realize that the pains of that autumn propelled me to open my heart to unconditional love. During this month, my physical and emotional pain motivated me to look deep within, become aware of the childhood wounds I was carrying, search for healing and meaning, connect with my heart and intuition, sit still, write, and set intentions for each day and for my life.

A month had gone by since I became ill with pneumonia, and I ached to run. I missed everything about it, the motion and the wind across my face, the adrenaline induced high, the scenic trails, and the tenderness of my tired muscles. I missed the feeling I had while running and afterwards. Running had been part of my routine before work. It brought a smile to my face and gave me the strength to deal with each day. One morning, even though my lung pain persisted, I decided to go for a 3-mile run, which was short for me. I was conditioned to run between eight and ten miles daily. It was dark and cold out, but I longed for the movement of feeling like I was flying. During the run, the pain increased in my left lower side where my left lung resides. It felt like a deep wound was living inside my lung tissue, but I kept going. I not only loved running, but I was addicted to it; I could not stop. When I returned from the run I started wheezing and could barely breathe. I had to work that day because I had used all of my allotted sick days. The long twelve hours of standing on my feet, answering pages, and caring for patients with a wide range of injuries and needs was very taxing on my weakened physical state. I took care of patients coming back from open-heart surgery, diagnosed with brain cancer, dying from COPD, in severe pain, and suffering from many other life-altering illnesses. On that October day, I barely made it to the end of my shift, the only thing keeping me alive being the connection I had with my patients.

There was a particular patient that day that touched my heart. He was diagnosed with COPD and was very short of breath. As he gasped for air, I could empathize completely. I knew what it was like to be in his shoes because I was wearing the same pair. He told me the medications were not helping, and again, I understood completely as my inhalers had not relieved my shortness of breath or wheezing either. He asked me what to do, and I said, "Pray." His eyes filled with tears, but I was somehow able to keep mine back. Later that day he gave me a postcard with a picture of a beautiful Native American woman. She had a white feather in her hair which reminded me of my delicate soul. He told me I was amazing and that I could do anything I wanted to in this life. I will never forget him or the gift he gave me. He gave me the strength to continue on my treacherous journey.

I was grieving the loss of running. My love of running began at the age of fourteen. By the time I was twenty-one, I was running collegiately. During my junior year of college, I dropped weight, my running times decreased, and I started hearing compliments on my looks for the first time in my life. I was becoming an excellent athlete, something I always strived to be. I attributed the fast running times and compliments to my thinness. My identity and self-esteem were dependent on my ability to run well and maintain a slim athletic physique. It was at this point that my childhood wounds had begun to manifest in the form of anorexia.

Not only did I try to run that particular October morning, but I also tried several mornings after. I was desperate to run. Each time I ran, I felt more ill, more short of breath, and more lung pain. It felt like the wound in my left lung was growing. It hurt to touch my left side, and I could not completely fill my left lung with air. At times I felt like I was suffocating. I was extremely anxious and terrified to gain weight because I was unable to run. I was fasting for days, eating only fruit for breakfast and skipping meals. My immune system was depleted. I had internalized the nasty comments of my childhood and did everything in my power to not be "too big" or "too tall." I controlled my food intake because I was terrified to gain even a pound. Subconsciously, gaining weight meant becoming a "gross giant" and never being loved. Being loved was ultimately what I was striving for.

Being called an ugly giant every day for several years during my childhood left a deep scar on my mind and body. Running brought me a false sense of safety, peace, and bliss. No matter how hard I tried, I could not run that fall. I was being faced with the challenge of confronting my deep-rooted childhood wounds. The future months and years would reveal the gifts I ultimately received from that fall.

I went to see a new doctor because of the intense and persistent left lung pain. This doctor took another chest x-ray and gave me a breathing test. He diagnosed me with severe asthma and put me on steroids. He was also a runner. I asked him when I would be able to run again, and he said by spring. He said while I am not running I should watch my calories so I would not gain weight. He reinforced my urge to maintain a strict diet. My anxiety heightened from the steroids and malnutrition. Anxiety is a common side effect of steroids. Also, low protein and low fat levels affect the brain which also causes an increase in anxiety. My illness worsened after that visit. The doctor only saw my asthma and pneumonia, and his recommendation to watch my calories was very harmful for me. He did not recognize that I had anorexia; neither did anyone else in Oregon, and neither did I.

I was getting worse each day, so I went to see an herbalist and nutritionist. The herbalist gave me a bottle of herbs to take daily, and the nutritionist recommended I stay away from wheat, dairy, and sugar and eat many fruits and vegetables. After following this advice, I became even more ill. I was dropping weight and was confused why my lungs were worsening. I was terrified. No one understood what I was enduring. I was all alone, in a dark cocoon, deepening my spiritual connection, opening my heart-space, and preparing for an extraordinary transformation.

My lung capacity was minimal; working twelve-hour shifts exhausted every cell in my body, and simply being able to breathe was at the forefront of my world. My pink running shorts and running shoes sat neglected at my front door. The days of running through green pastures, under vivid blue skies, and over glistening streams seemed long gone. Barely could I remember what it felt like to have full lung capacity. I could literally feel the wound within my lung tissues growing each day. I was living with severe lung pain, panic, and shortness of breath day in and day out. Chronic inflammation from severe asthma, panic, and malnourishment delayed the healing process. Questions flooded my mind. How long would this last? Would I ever fully heal? How long would the pain continue? When would I be able to take a full breath? What would I do with my life now? Who was I really?

Before I became ill, I was known as a runner. My friends were runners, I ran every day, I shopped at the running store, and I wore running shoes. My life was centered on running, being in nature, and maintaining a thin frame. My home was on the running trails. Running brought me to remote places within nature that gave me that sense of love I longed to feel. Nature recognized me and I felt unconditionally loved and accepted on the trails. My happiness and peace of mind was dictated by my ability to run. After trying to run several times that fall and becoming increasingly ill with each run, I realized I had to let go of running. I simply could not run. I started to feel depressed, lonely, and like the ugly giant I was called in junior high. I was barely eating or breathing. My home, the running trails, and my body were disappearing.

Maureen, a gentle, kind woman, came to me when I needed her the most. One fall day I was working at the hospital and feeling very short of breath. I entered the break room to get my inhaler, and Maureen, a registered nurse, sat there munching on her morning snack and asked me how I was. I told her I was short of breath and my left lower side was in severe pain near where my lung was. Maureen believed in the ancient healing powers of Epsom salt baths, and she invited me to enjoy Epsom salt baths in her home, as I did not have a bathtub in mine.

After a long twelve-hour shift at the hospital, my lungs were exhausted and painful. I drove to Maureen's home. That night and for many nights to follow I took Epsom salt baths and spoke with this wise woman. Hearing about her journey of healing and self-discovery gave me more strength and wisdom to walk through my own journey. She gave me books, herbs, bath salts, and a gentle heart to reach for in a rocky time. She referred me to an extraordinary healer, Dr. Katherine, a woman who changed my life. Because this healer lived far away, I made an appointment with her for a phone session. I waited eagerly for my appointment.

Late that fall rain came to the valley; humidity filled the air, yet the inflammation and phlegm persisted in my lung tissues. My days were filled with Epsom salt baths, herbs, inhalers, medicines, daily meditations, prayer, angels, butterflies, and inner reflections. When I meditated, I felt my heart-space. It felt warm and loving. It felt as though my heart was trying to emerge and expand. I could feel incredible sensations within and around my heart, sensations of tingling, opening, and heat. Butterflies surrounded me constantly that year and in years to follow. They landed on my shoes. They came to me in times of need and in times of joy. They were messengers from the divine. I felt a sense of belonging with the butterflies.

On a sunny fall day, I dialed the phone of Dr. Katherine, energy worker, intuitive, and naturopath. Eagerness and excitement filled my body when a peaceful, gentle voice answered the phone, "How can we help?" Dr. Katherine channeled a group of beings called Guidance. They were high vibration beings (angels and ascended masters) that could read energy and answer deeply personal questions. After an hour of phone conversation, my life began to change. I gained a new perspective. As the rain washed away the fog in the valley, I was becoming clearer about my inner purpose and my true gifts. During my phone conversation with Dr. Katherine, Guidance told me I was sick for a very specific purpose. They told me I was learning unconditional love for myself. They said my soul had come to this planet to embody unconditional love, and learning self-love was an important step on my path. All my life I had been searching for love and acceptance outside of myself, and it was now time to learn it from within. They suggested I keep a self-love journal and begin writing a list every morning of things I appreciate about myself. They said it was very important to monitor each thought I have and chose loving thoughts. They told me my thoughts affect my energy field, my body, and my reality. They told me my soul had come to Earth to help awaken humanity and part of my journey was learning unconditional love, divine love, love that is beyond height, weight, skin, and flesh; true, non-judgmental love. They also told me that I was here to live in an awakened state of bliss, and through this illness I would completely awaken and live from my soul's true perspective. They also told me my chakras (the body's centers of spiritual powers) and energy fields were starting to open, and in three to four years I would be able to channel very strong healing energy. They told me I had extraordinary healing gifts and that I was a healer and a teacher.

This information was both wonderful and frightening. Dr. Katherine validated what I had always felt since a child; I was here for a higher purpose. I had always known that I had an inner calling. Yet, I was terrified to awaken to it. Would others judge my spiritual and healing gifts? Could I really awaken to my gifts? I did not want to be seen as weird, like I was as a child and teen. I desperately wanted to feel accepted by others, yet I knew I had a strong calling of the heart.

That day on the phone with Dr. Katherine I realized that this lung illness was a gateway to my calling. My inner calling of love and service started to become reality. From that day forward I was able to see more clearly than ever before that I was here for a purpose, and health and bliss were my natural states of being.

I started to listen to a song about the courage to stand in your light. I listened to this song daily during my breaks at work, in the morning, and at night. The focus of my life began to shift from being depressed because I could not run and was ill, to cultivating the light within and unconditional love for myself. Guidance gave me the motivation to look deeper within my inner workings.

I started a self-love journal that fall. I wrote things that I appreciated about myself. I painted daily affirmation cards that read "my life is balanced, my lungs are healed, and I am gentle and loving with myself." I posted loving messages all around my home. I was training my mind to think loving thoughts, and I was learning how to love myself.

I spent more time journaling, meditating, and questioning the world around me. I began to feel that serving my heart and my inner calling was my main focus in life, rather than running. I still feared gaining weight and kept myself on a restricted diet, but I slowly started to let go of running. Left-sided lung pain, anorexia, panic, and shortness of breath continued to dominate my physical state, but my internal world was changing. I spent time alone in nature sitting under the trees and watching the birds, journaling, reading, and getting in touch with my heart. I was planting internal seeds of resilience, love, radiance, compassion, joy and forgiveness. I began to question why I was here and what I really wanted from life. As my physical body weakened, my internal state began strengthening. At times I thought I might die from my physical condition, but I knew I had a higher purpose, a calling that kept me alive. I missed having full lung capacity and running through mystical trails, but my deep longing to serve a higher purpose gave me the strength I needed to face the physical limitations. It was in the quiet moments of feeling my heart and connecting with nature where I found the grace and courage to face my present life challenge.

As I forgive myself, learn to love my shortcomings, and speak from my heart, I am reminded of the connection between the river, the roses, the butterflies, the eagles, and all living things.

Chapter 3

The Magic of Snowflakes

It was the month of December. Cold air filled the valley floor, lights covered the streets of Ashland, and Christmas carols could be heard throughout the town. My left-sided lung pain continued, and my weakened state of being kept me inside away from the cold and crowds. I spent most of my time meditating, connecting with my heart, listening to inspirational music, and wondering if I would ever be able to fully breathe again.

That year I made plans to visit my family in Minnesota for Christmas. Most young athletes recover from pneumonia within weeks or months, but my renewal took longer. Mine was a journey of awakening and transforming into a crystalline state like a caterpillar transforms into a butterfly. I wondered how I would be able to relay this to my family and friends.

I always had powerful women come into my life when I needed them most, and that winter a marvelous friend was there. Her name was Dena. I had met her at Joyful Yoga in Jacksonville, Oregon during the fall of 2008. We had been practicing yoga, chanting, meditation, and learning about Reiki (an ancient healing system using universal guided energy), energy fields, energetic cords, and chakras with Louise Lavergne. Louise is a Reiki Master, yoga teacher, author, and owner of Joyful Yoga, and she created a program called Yoga-On-The-Go. Joyful Yoga was located in a small, cozy studio. The outside looked like a log cabin and the inside had beautiful wooden floors. I discovered Joyful Yoga one day after coming back from a long run.

There were fifteen miles of mountain running trails outside the back door of my apartment in Jacksonville, Oregon. Jacksonville was a town of only 2,800 nestled neatly in a valley. Trails and mountains surrounded the main avenue. Joyful Yoga was located on a street parallel to the main avenue and was two minutes running distance from my apartment. As I was coming back from a ten-mile mountain run that day, the sign for Joyful Yoga stood out and I decided to stop into the studio. At that time in my life I had practiced some Vinyasa Yoga, but I did not meditate nor did I know anything about energy fields or Reiki. As I opened the old wooden door, a woman with vibrant red hair, large, clear blue eyes, and creative clothing introduced herself to me as Louise Lavergne. I felt as though I had known this woman for years as we began chatting. I felt safe and at home right away in her intimate studio. Within the next several days I attended one of Louise's yoga classes. The class was like no other yoga class I had attended. Louise called it Kundalini Yoga, but I think of it as magical yoga. During the class we did a lot of deep breathing, chanting, meditating, and postures that realign one's energy field. The music was vibrant and it took me to a place I had not previously been. After class the three other students, Louise, and I gathered to have tea. We chatted about our busy lives, spiritual phenomena, and, of course, boys. After only this first class I had already found a home away from home. I began attending Louise's Kundalini Yoga classes weekly. Then, I began going to Louise for private consultations. She became my spiritual guide and Reiki teacher. She assigned me certain chants to do in the morning to assist with my spiritual awakening. Louise came into my life when I was becoming ready to learn about energetic fields and to spiritually grow.

As time progressed Louise became a significant figure in my world. I often went to her studio three times a week. I thought very highly of her, and I followed her guidance. If she told me to chant for fifteen minutes every morning, I would. I truly believed she was helping me awaken to my soul purpose, and I trusted her.

My relationship with Louise also lead to another woman I would soon be deeply connected to. Dena entered my life after my good friend, Brooke, died in a tragic mountaineering accident in the spring of 2008. The day after Brooke died, I went to Joyful Yoga for a meditation and Kundalini Yoga class with Louise, and Dena was there in the front row. After class Dena and I were sipping tea and getting to know each other. Dena asked me what my plans were for the weekend, and I began crying and explained to her that I would be attending Brooke's funeral. Dena had felt this loss in times past and was able provide sincere support and compassion. I was able to process my dear friend's tragic death with the support of Dena, Louise, yoga and meditation, and a power greater than me. After meeting Dena, studying with Louise, and experiencing Brooke's death, I began to sense things that I had not previously sensed. For example, one day while driving I was thinking of Brooke. Within minutes of thinking that she must still be close by, a beautiful rainbow appeared. It was stunningly bright and brought a smile to my face. That gorgeous rainbow will stay with me forever.

Dena and I bonded over the following several months. The summer before my illness, Dena and I lounged in the garden, hiked on the trails around Mt. Shasta, chatted about ex-lovers, swam in the Lithia Park Lake, and made late night dinners together. That fall and winter she stood close by as I consulted with her on different herbs, inhalers, medicines, bath salts, vitamins, and healers. Dena was well-known in the Ashland community through her work at a center for natural healing, and she assisted me in every way she could. Dena always provided an open ear and heart when I was going through difficult times. Our friendship was divinely orchestrated.

During Christmas of 2009, Dena and I were meeting for sushi to exchange gifts. It was cold, and I was wearing jeans and a pink sweater beneath a purple, wool pea coat. My neck was wrapped in a delicate, white fleece scarf. I did not like breathing the cold air so I always wrapped my neck and mouth with a warm scarf. As I was walking down the streets of Ashland to meet Dena, I felt different from the people passing by on the street. As I watched others converse about their daily lives, I conversed with my angels and my heart. Most of the humans I saw around me spent their time focusing on earthly matters, but I spent my time focusing within my heart and on my angels. My external condition forced me to look inward. Not many people understood what I was going through. I was in a cocoon. I was facing my fears, looking deep within, changing my perspective, and ultimately connecting with my heart and soul.

As soon as I opened the door to the restaurant, I saw Dena sitting in a booth waiting for me. I walked over to her and she greeted me with a massive hug. We started catching up on our days, our epiphanies, our journeys, and our boy stories. I told Dena about a guy from my past that had reentered my life for one date. We talked about letting go of the past and embracing the future. I told her I was having a very difficult time letting go of running, staying in the moment, and finding my internal happiness and peace. Dena understood; she had love and compassion for me.

I talked to Dena about everything, except my anorexia. That I hid from the world and myself. It was a shameful secret that was eating me alive. I was terrified of gaining weight. I already felt enormous standing at six feet tall, and I did not want to be tall and wide. I did everything I could to shrink myself. I wanted to disappear; I wanted to be petite. Ultimately, I wanted to be lovable. I wanted to be accepted, not shunned. I did not want to stand out when I entered a room. I was deeply hurt by the daily "wow, you are so tall" comments. I was barely eating. My stomach was in constant pain, and I would often fast. I experienced daily panic attacks. I did not feel safe in my body or in the world. I read about detoxification and told myself I was detoxifying my lung illness. My immunity was struggling and my nervous system was out of balance. I felt like a giant even though I was underweight. I had deep body shame and did not yet know how to nourish and love myself physically, mentally, emotionally, or spiritually. I continued to write in my self-love journal and practice daily affirmations. I was learning a new way that took time. I was learning unconditional love for myself and my body. Starting when I was a young child, I had received comments daily regarding my height. I had not yet learned how to deflect those comments, and they went deep within. They ate away at my insides. My organs were suffering. I was in a dark cocoon. That Christmas Dena gave me a gift that stayed with me through my dark cocoon phase into my butterfly emergence.

After much talking Dena and I exchanged gifts. I handed her a package wrapped in gold and she handed me a package wrapped in white. I watched her carefully open the package. She took the tape off as though she was handling a butterfly's delicate wing. When she got to the center of the package there was a small box for her to open. Her eyes glistened. Dena has beautiful clear blue eyes that sparkle. She opened the white box and inside she found a clear crystal attached to a silver cord which made a stunning necklace. She put it on and told me, "This is just what I need, a necklace to liberate my femininity." Dena and I are warrior goddesses and stewards of the divine feminine emergence. I explained to her that the stone carried energetic properties that vibrate at the frequency of unconditional love. She graciously thanked me. Then I began to open my white package. With eagerness and excitement I peeled off the layers of tissue paper. It was a bowl full of angelic beauty. It sparkled; white wings and feathers surrounded the entire white bowl, and it carried a special energy, one of hope. I listened intently to her explain the road she traveled to obtain this bowl – it was truly a bowl of magic. She told me that she had gone to Sound Peace to get this bowl, which was the same store where I purchased her necklace. She explained to me that one day when she was shopping, she entered Sound Peace, saw this bowl, and thought of me instantly. She went to purchase the bowl for me, and after getting home she found that the cashier had put a different white bowl in the box. At first Dena thought, this isn't the bowl I chose, but it is pretty, and I can give this one to Alexandra instead. But that night she had a dream about the bowl, and when she awoke in the morning she just knew it was not the bowl to give me. She went back to Sound Peace and found the original bowl she had wanted to give me. There was only one left and she knew that was the one. Months later the beauty of this bowl was revealed to me again when I was in Mt. Shasta at an energy healer's home.

As we left that night Dena explained to me that she envisioned business cards with my name on them lying inside the bowl.

Previously, I had spoken with Dena about my dreams of pursuing my inner calling and becoming a Reiki healer and teacher. The angelic bowl became a symbol of my dreams.

The next morning I meditated by a bright candle and set intentions for a safe trip to Minnesota for Christmas. My flight left at eleven on the morning of December 23, 2009, and it took all the strength I had to make it to the airport. While onboard and preparing for take-off, I became short of breath. I closed my eyes and asked my angels to help me make it through the flight safely, which I did. I landed in Minnesota that evening. My brother greeted me at the baggage claim. I was very anxious to see him. Even though I had spoken with my mother often on the phone, I had not updated her or the rest of my family on how sick I truly was. I did not want them to know. I had always been very strong, athletic, healthy, and energetic. I feared that if my family knew how sick I was they would be very frightened, have misperceptions, and judge me.

Once my bags had arrived at the baggage claim, my brother helped me take them to the car, and then we headed to our childhood home in Minnetonka, Minnesota. I felt exhausted, anxious, and short of breath upon arriving at my parents' home. My parents greeted me with hugs. They loved me the very best they knew how. Their home smelled of pine from the beautiful real Christmas tree, fresh baked bread my father had just taken out of the oven, cinnamon from mother's candles, and sweet potatoes which my mother had baked for dinner. Food was everywhere, and I was anxious. I was scared to eat, and I feared receiving my family's concerned comments saying, "You are too skinny and not eating." My anorexia was the elephant in the room, and I felt shame and fear around it which contributed to my restrictive behavior.

That evening I headed downstairs to my childhood bedroom to unload my bags and tuck myself in for the night. As I lay on my childhood bed, I put one hand on my heart and one hand on my belly and prayed to my angels for healing. I drifted off to sleep with tears in my eyes.

I awoke early the next morning, Christmas Eve Day, to meditate and spend time in my childhood room which had four windows overlooking the forest and the swing set in the backyard. My parents lived on a property that was filled with beautiful trees; the backyard was a mystical forest. There were many deer, wild turkeys, eagles, and rabbits on their property. That morning I set intentions for healing, peace, and happiness.

After meditating I made my way upstairs. My father was making pancakes, my mother was doing her qigong exercises, and my brother was reading the newspaper. As I greeted my family, the smell of food made me anxious. My stomach hurt. I did not eat much for breakfast that morning, and my mother and brother looked at me with concern in their eyes. My father was in his own world, a world of denial. I began to feel nauseated from the fear in the room and lack of communication. I took it all within as I had always done. I swallowed the family's fear. As my left lung began to fill with pain, I forced my tears back.

That evening we had Christmas Eve dinner. When I sat down to see the huge portion of food in front of me, I became very short of breath. Thoughts flooded my mind: "I am too anxious to eat and my stomach hurts. I do not want any of this food, it will hurt my lungs and vibration." I learned in Oregon that each food holds a certain energetic vibration, and I became frightened to eat any foods with a low vibration. I was also afraid of any foods that could be harmful for the lungs and difficult for the stomach to digest. I thought, "My family does not understand me or my process. They are judging me for not eating." I ate a few bites and swallowed the fearful looks. It was a challenging Christmas Eve for me.

After dinner my brother appeared sad and terrified. My heart went out to him. Even though my brother had judged and hurt me as a little girl, I had deep compassion, forgiveness and love for him. When he was sad I did everything I could to help him.

That evening I talked with my brother separate from our parents. He began crying. He said, "Mom and Dad do not understand me, no one does, and I am totally alone." My brother completely broke down. I had never seen him like that before. He was sobbing. I began to feel my heart expand and profound love came over me for him and his situation. I asked my angels to help him, and I felt immense light within and all around me. He began to soften. I had deep empathy for him. I imagined much love and light filling him, my parents, and my parents' home. I asked my angels for assistance with healing within my family.

My brother and I talked for several hours about our family and upbringing. I listened to him explain how lonely his childhood was. I listened with great empathy, yet I was still unable to open up about myself. I was still in my cocoon and scared of his misperceptions. I had not yet learned how to shine the love and light onto myself, heal myself, and transcend my childhood.

I will never forget Christmas morning that year. I awoke to enormous, magical snowflakes falling outside my childhood bedroom window. Despite my lung illness and family concerns, that Christmas morning I was able to find peace and joy in nature. The snowflakes outside my childhood bedroom ignited the love within my heart, and I wanted to share the magic of nature with others. I ran upstairs. My father was there; we were the only two early birds that morning. Enthusiasm and a high energy level were traits I had inherited from my father. I said, "Dad, let's go out in the snow." Even though my lung pain persisted, I wanted to experience the magical morning in nature. We bundled up with me wearing every layer I had, and we ventured outside. I was in awe of the wondrous snowflakes all around me. My lung illness had forced me to slow down to the point where I noticed the smallest details of life. I was alone in my cocoon, but nature understood me. Nature felt like my friend, and so did the snowflakes.

My father and I did not get very far on our Christmas morning walk until my lungs started screaming in pain. I was carrying a bag of fluid, pus, mucous, and blood within my lung tissues. I could never take a full breath and my lungs were always in pain. Even with minimal exercise the pain was excruciating. As I sat in my dark cocoon separated from the outer world, sacs of fluid sagged within my saturated lung tissues. The heavy shame and secrecy of anorexia sat close to my heart. I was not yet able to break through my cocoon and speak my truth.

That Christmas I realized the magic of snowflakes. The light delicacy and beauty of each individual snowflake that I saw on the walk with my father made me smile. My illness had shown me a new perspective. It slowed the pace of my entire life and allowed me to see the beauty in simple things like snowflakes. From my struggle through an illness that diminished my lung capacity and gave such pain, I discovered that finding pleasure in simplicities kept me alive.

As I begin to trust the process, flow with grace, and accept what is, my heart-space begins to open like a beautiful pink rose. As I begin to align with my truth, listen deeply, see others with eyes of compassion, and speak with courage, my wings start to sparkle and my body begins to feel free.

CHAPTER 4

Close to My Heart

For a year I had been making trips to the sacred Mount Shasta. The mountain intrigued me, inspired me, and called me to come to her. I had already made plans to climb it that spring with my father. Deep down I knew I wouldn't be well enough to do it so soon, but hope prevailed. Every time I visited the magical mountain my heart fluttered, visions came to mind, and opportunities seemed limitless. When I saw her in January 2010, my heart began to fill with sensations of warmth, lightness, and expansion. I knew this mountain had much truth to reveal to me.

It was always an adventure going into Berryville, the health food market in Mt. Shasta. Each person in the small market had a unique story to share. Some women were covered in hemp clothing, others wore designer clothes from top to bottom; some had dreadlocks, others had fake eyelashes; some wore bright red lipstick, and some wore no makeup at all. I appreciated this market greatly because one could truly be her own woman there. You could wear as radiant clothing or ragged outdoor gear as you chose and still be embraced. I loved this atmosphere for I am the type of woman who wears running shorts with mud splattered up and down her legs some days and other days a beautiful pink lace dress with gold shoes. Berryville is a place that supports each person's inner beauty.

That January I drove to Mt. Shasta to see an energy healer, Beloved Heartsong. As I made the hour long drive, I could see the mountain far off in the distance, glowing. It looked like white light was radiating from the snow-covered peaks. As I listened to Snatam Kaur (a musical artist who I chant to every morning, have met in person, and adore and cherish deeply), I felt my heart opening. The closer I came to the mountain, the more I felt energetic sensations of warmth and palpitations within my heart-space. When I arrived on the main street of Mt. Shasta, I made a left hand turn towards the home of Beloved. I found her home, parked my car, and walked towards the front door. She greeted me with a tight embrace. Her humility, warmth, character, and love eased my nerves. After entering her peaceful home she invited me to take a seat on the couch. I filled out some paperwork as she finished preparing the healing space. She then assisted me to lie on her healing table. It was soft, comfortable and warm. Relaxing music played softly in the background. She covered me in a white blanket and then asked if I was comfortable enough. I said, "Yes," and she then started the healing session. She began by placing her hands on my forehead. I closed my eyes and drifted in and out. I felt energetic sensations of warmth and lightness throughout my body. When she placed her hands on my heart, I felt it expand and radiate. Sensations of warmth filled my entire heart-space. I sensed several hands on me at once, as if there were many healers in the room with me. My hands and feet were unusually warm. At the end of the session I felt huge waves of energy circle around and through me.

After the healing session, she shared her visions with me. She revealed that at the beginning of the session, she saw and heard an enormous white angel standing behind me saying, "Alexandra, Alexandra – you are pure and beautiful" (I was in the midst of changing my name from Ali to Alexandra, and I have since come to realize the name Alexandra is the energetic vibration of my soul). Then, she saw a doe's face (a symbol of gentleness) licking me and communicating with me; there were many deer and animals of the woods all around me. She explained that as she touched my lungs she felt surges of energy pouring from her fingers into my lungs. When she touched my shoulders she envisioned a huge eagle swoop in with a loud screech, and it was at that moment that she heard birds in the familiar music piece playing that she had never heard before. I have since come to realize my profound connection with eagles. She then saw that I was on a train. I opened the door to usher hundreds of people onboard. Finally, she saw blue and white light encircling my field and pouring through me. She explained that my session was filled with a lot of white light, which symbolizes initiation. She said that I was in the midst of an initiation into the Light. She told me I was awakening to my true essence.

As I was leaving her home, I saw the angelic bowl; it was the same bowl Dena had given me for Christmas. My eyes glistened as I stared into the bowl. She asked me if I would like one of the quotes from the bowl. I reached in with delight and picked a quote. It read "you are now ready for the life you always wanted." An enormous sensation of excitement filled my body. I left her home that day fully onboard with my soul calling.

For a week after the healing session I felt light, free, and expansive, and my lung pain was nearly gone. I felt so wonderful that I thought I could start running again. I hadn't let go of my addiction to running yet. I tried to run one sunny morning through the country fields of Ashland, Oregon. When I returned from the run, my lung pain came back worse than ever, and my ability to breathe diminished greatly. It felt like both my lungs were filled with fluid.

After that run I was feeling very short of breath, anxious, in pain, and exhausted. I had not yet made the connection between my lung pain and anxiety with my anorexia. My system was malnourished and in a constant state of panic. I was terrified to gain weight. I was sad and scared and I did not know who to turn to. I called my father. I started sobbing on the phone.

"Dad, I don't think I'll ever be able to be active again. My lungs are in such bad condition. How can I go on? I can't even walk to the grocery store without becoming short of breath and my lungs throbbing in pain."

My father said, "Alexandra, you can do this. I know you can get through this. You have climbed the mountains in Patagonia, passed your nursing boards, and overcome tremendous challenges from your youth. I know you can achieve whatever you put your mind to."

I said, "But, dad, what am I going to do with myself, I can't even walk well right now."

"Paint," my father replied. "You are an artist like me, and you loved painting in your college days. Get back into it."

After that phone conversation I went to the cupboard and gathered all my art supplies. I found a variety of paints, my old easel, sketchbooks, canvases, paintbrushes, and glass jars. The bright colors, the canvases and the beautiful paintbrushes enchanted me. I was instantly reminded of how much I love painting.

My most remarkable painting was of an African man I painted in college. As a five-year-old I had spiritual visions of traveling to Africa. In high school I had a strong desire to be in Africa, but my dream was crushed by my mother. She said, "Africa is not safe and too far away." I knew Africa was very close to me in my heart. Due to subliminal messages from my family and society, I suppressed my desire to travel to Africa. My deep desire to be in Africa was stuffed into a deep dark box throughout my childhood and into my college years. But my paintings always revealed my soul. As I began to heal and emerge from my dark cocoon, I came to realize my desire to travel to Africa was no accident. It was part of my soul.

During February 2010 I spent my spare time painting butterflies. I painted huge radiant wings and colorful images. I painted blue, pink, yellow, and orange butterflies. I rushed home from work every day to finish a painting. Even though I could hardly breathe, I began to feel joy again. I loved the feeling of colors gliding off my paintbrushes, and I felt great satisfaction after I finished a beautiful painting. I remembered my days in college when I was an art major and how much I loved the painting studio. That spring I signed up for a painting class; I met a painting teacher and made new friends. My creativity was blossoming once again. I began spending most of my spare time and extra money on art.

One night I had a dream of a huge, beautiful, blue and green butterfly. I saw all the intricacies of the butterfly's wings in the dream. The dream was vivid, mystical and magical. I sensed the butterfly came to me in my dream state to reassure me that I would eventually heal and to tell me I was going through a transformation just as the butterfly does. That dream gave me the courage to continue on my path.

After painting a series of butterflies, I painted my favorite flower, the rose. That winter I developed a connection with roses. I started buying roses weekly to treat myself. I sensed the energy within the roses. The roses were speaking to my heart just as my angels did. Sometimes the roses would bloom beautifully and stay alive for a month in my home. Each rose was unique, having a different shade and aura, and staying alive for a different length of time. When I would buy a rose I could feel the sensation in my heart expand. I have learned that roses hold the same energetic property as the heart chakra. Roses represent unconditional love.

That winter I had canvases lined up along my entire cottage studio and brushes in every corner. My home was becoming an art studio and I loved it. Every morning when I woke, I would turn on beautiful music, meditate, and go within my heart-space. I would put on my painting apron and paint on a large canvas using bright, playful colors. I was falling in love with art all over again.

My wooden table from Ethiopia held all my art supplies. The table traveled with me all the way from Portland, Oregon. I had bought the table with my mother the day I had moved into my first apartment. I picked it because it was handmade in Ethiopia and the money went to supporting the women and children of Africa. On my table I had eleven different acrylic paints lying out, a jar from college which held my water, a small blue book called "Heal Your Body" by Louise Hay, a picture of an African child I had seen in the newspaper, and two quotes, one saying "we are spiritual beings having a human experience," by Pierre Teilhard de Chardin, and the other said "we can do anything we want to if we stick to it long enough" by Helen Keller. My wooden table and the belongings it held brought me comfort and joy that cold, dark winter.

On my drive home from work, birds would line up along the telephone wires. There would be thousands of birds awaiting my arrival at my country cottage. They would be in the trees, on my roof, in the bushes, all over. Spirit and the natural world were calling me to awaken to the light of my soul. I was shifting my energy and being propelled to live in a new vibration; a vibration of freedom and light, similar to the vibration of the butterfly. Spirit was calling me to transcend as a butterfly does. The quote I received from the energy healer's bowl, "you are now ready for the life you always wanted," meant that I was now ready for the life my soul has always wanted: to be completely awake. I was in the process of awakening.

My connection with nature, animals, and the spiritual world was growing stronger each day. Painting became a form of meditation for me. It quieted my mind and allowed the stillness and unconditional love of my heart to surface. I was feeling my inner calling and connection to my soul more deeply than ever before. I felt closer to the spiritual world than the earthly world.

My connection with nature was growing extremely strong. I would awake in the morning and there would be flocks upon flocks of birds flying in circles all around my cottage, chirping and screeching. I could feel the presence of the trees, I could sense when the birds were trying to communicate with me, and I could understand the messages they sent. By April the weather was warming, and I felt free to go outside. When the weather was warm I was not as worried about my lungs as I walked through Lithia Park. I would walk to a quiet, pristine spot in the park by the river, and I would paint and write in my self-love journal. I continued to write loving affirmations about myself. I painted pictures that read "I am safe, I am healed, I am balanced, and I am beautiful." I would gaze at the sparkling, blue river. I listened to the birds singing and the trees blowing in the wind. As I dangled my feet in and out of the water, I would often see a butterfly come to rest on my foot. Nature and butterflies brought me hope that my lungs would fully recover. That spring I spent as much time as I could in nature. My lung pain was still intense, and I was still short of breath and underweight, but I felt a sense of hope by my connection with the birds, the river, the clouds, the rocks, the trees, the butterflies and the deer.

I was learning a new way to commune with nature. A way that was silent and inward, rather than active and outward. I would watch the birds; the gentleness, grace, and freedom of their wings reminded me of my own heartbeat. The delicacies and intricacies of their wings reminded me of the sensitivity of my lungs. Each bird I saw delivered a special message that I felt within the deep layers of my own inner workings. I was learning the beauty and grace of stillness. I missed running through the trails, but I knew wisdom was emerging within me, and I was willing to let go of competitive running for the calling of my soul and the greater whole.

It seemed the birds and I were becoming one. I saw birds in singles, pairs, and groupings, some were small, others large. They continued to line up on the telephone wires on my way home from work. They would sing to me. I would see them outside the window of a patient's room at the hospital. I saw them when I was standing at a wedding. I saw them while on a walk behind my childhood home in Minnesota. Sometimes they would fly right next to my bedroom window, sometimes they would walk next to me in the park, and other times they would soar high above me while I was walking down the street. They came with me everywhere I went. Every time I saw them, whether individually or as a group, I was reminded of my own freedom and grace.

My daily experiences at the hospital began to reveal my healing gifts, and my life began changing. I had always been interested in medicine, the body, and healing, but now a certain type of healing beyond the mind was developing within my heart. When I was in a patient's room, my body would fill with warmth and my hands would heat up. As I touched my patients with the warmth of my hands, my whole body would sweat. Sometimes I would be dripping with sweat. Often the patient's pain would resolve, and their anxiety would diminish. On one occasion, a patient revealed to me their deepest fears and cried uncontrollably. One patient's wound stopped bleeding completely. One time a hospice patient died very peacefully while the healing energy flowed through my body. As my healing abilities were developing, many patients in the hospital were reaping the benefits.

I started to see the spark and connection within all living things. My love for nature, animals, and art grew stronger. The beauty of the sky, the gentleness of the birds, and the rhythms of the river spoke to my heart, and I listened. I was developing a communication with my heart, my soul, and the spirit world.

I was able to feel my heart's messages. My heart would guide me towards a situation or a person through sensations of warmth, expansion, and pulsating rhythms. My life was changing day by day; my wings were emerging and meditation was a constant. I started to see the pain in my lungs as a gift, an opportunity to expand and develop my wings, and to align myself with my heart, angels, and the light within. The lungs are the organs closest to Spirit. In many spiritual traditions it is said the presence of Spirit comes through the breath. I was starting to understand that aligning with Spirit, my soul, and my heart was the gift of my lung illness.

I started to attend a weekly spiritual talk held by Pia Smith Orleane and Cullen Baird Smith, extraordinary interstellar communicators. Pia and Cullen state, "that the information they share comes from an energetic merging of their hearts and minds to the hearts and minds of other Light Beings who wish to help humanity evolve." They communicate with a group of Light Beings called Laarkmaa. Laarkmaa's messages are about following one's heart-space and living from the vibration of love. Their talks validated my spiritual experiences. Laarkmaa revealed to me that I was in the process of developing a sacred communication with my heart. These messages were validating and healing. My connection to my heart, my soul, and the spirit world was growing stronger every day. Pia and Cullen were a strong source of hope and light for me during a very trying time.

Flash forward to 2015: *I am grateful for the many healers and teachers that have guided me home to my heart and soul on my path of awakening. I always had treasures of light, hope, inspiration, and powerful healers in my sphere.*

That summer my mother found a letter that I wrote to her when I had traveled to Belize and stayed with a local family in the jungle. She gave me the letter to read. In that letter I had written: *"The more I travel, the more I see the unity of the world. I see the world as a whole and each person, each culture, each medicine representing an important section. I feel that living sustainably with the earth in a way that humans can thrive requires the integration of western science and traditional spirituality."* After reading this section, I recognized that what I wrote five years ago rang even more true today. The physical and the spiritual are complements of each other and when integrated as a whole, sustainable living can be achieved. I was integrating the spiritual into my daily life that year, but I had lost touch with physical reality in many ways, and it would not be for several years until my physical being would become grounded and whole. That summer the magic of nature, meditation, art, and animals gave me hope, while my physical body was depleted, short of breath, and in pain.

As I review the past, embrace the present, and look forward to the future, possibilities seem limitless. Dreams, fantasies, and mountain views seem too real to be true. The belief that I am free, the trust that I know myself, and the wisdom to allow my heart-space to guide gives me the strength to continue on the journey.

CHAPTER 5

The Beauty of a Broken Wing

It was the fall of 2010. My severe lung pain persisted, I was short of breath and extremely anxious, and I was still struggling with a very poor body image and restrictive food behaviors. The heavy body shame I felt and my childhood wounds were imbedded deep within my subconscious. I carried these wounds within my lung tissues. I have come to learn that much of our thoughts and behaviors are subconscious until we bring more light to them, and I was in a process of peeling away my subconscious layers, like the layers of an onion are peeled, until the pure light in the center can be revealed.

My physical limitations slowed me down enough to allow the veils to begin lifting. Eagles came to me that year as divine messengers, and I was aware enough to see them as such. That fall I had an incredible encounter with a patient at the hospital that reminded me of my deep connection to eagles. I was preparing to start a new IV on an older gentleman who was healing from knee surgery. I was engaging fully with him and after several minutes of talking he told me that I reminded him of birds. I was delighted to hear this. I smiled with sparkles in my eyes and told him, "thank you; I love birds." I shared with him my experience of seeing two eagles fly in front of my car on the drive back from Mt. Ashland.

Flashback: *It was springtime, the flowers were blooming, and my mother was in town. I was not able to go hiking with my mother this spring due to my lung injury, so we decided to take a drive to the mountains instead. We drove up to Mt. Ashland. When we arrived at the top, the mountains and trails were all around me as far as I could see. My heart began to ache for I was heartbroken that I could not go hiking, mountain climbing, or running through this beauty. We sat at the top of the mountain soaking in the nature all around us. Tears filled my eyes. I felt like a piece of me was missing, broken, and in need of healing. We spent several minutes sitting in the car at the base of Mt. Ashland before we decided to drive back down. I drove my car down the mountain slowly for there were still tears in my eyes and part of my heart felt shattered. As I was driving through the winding road with towering trees all around us, two eagles suddenly appeared soaring directly in front of the car. We were driving in my new convertible beetle, the color of the sky, with the top down. It was a magnificent sight. The beautiful eagles were magical, gentle, and graceful. My heart filled with light, and something inside told me I would fully heal.*

The gentleman I was attending to went on to tell me about his knowledge of eagles and their beauty. He said that the most beautiful eagles he had seen were the ones who had recovered from a broken wing. He explained that they had been tamed and they were extremely gentle creatures. My heart began to radiate and expand as I made the connection between the eagle's broken wing and my broken lung. My lung illness was taming me. I was learning to be still, love myself, be gentle with myself, and go within my heart-space.

That year eagles came to me often. I would be in the park and see graceful eagles flying in circles above me. The eagles reminded me to see beyond my lung pain and see the magnificence of my awakening journey. They reminded me to keep my thoughts in alignment with my heart. Their messages were about divine love and courage.

A week after my encounter with the patient at the hospital, I met two feline friends who brought me an abundance of hope, joy, and unconditional love. On a sunny afternoon late in November, my friend Wendy called me to see if I wanted to go the humane society with her. Years ago I had wanted an orange cat, but this thought had not returned to me recently. I agreed with excitement.

When we arrived at the humane society we asked where the kittens were. A woman named Rose told us they only had three kittens left. They were all from the same litter and were all orange. She took us over to the cage and opened it up. I saw one, named Moe, and immediately wanted to hold him. Within seconds I decided he was mine. I instantly fell in love with his sweet, gentle, playful, warm nature. She said he had been with his brother Larry since birth and it would be best if they stayed together, so I decided to buy Moe and Larry both. I did not question my deep desire to take them home with me. I knew from the minute I laid eyes on Moe he was a part of my soul. I took them home within ten minutes. My friend bought Curly, the third kitten from the litter. Moe and Larry warmed my heart from that day on. The sound of their purr soothed my emotions, their tiny pink noses made me smile, their unconditional love taught me how to love myself, and their playful nature brought out mine. They filled my world with so much love during such a trying time in my life. That was the beginning of my realization of the profound healing power of animals.

I was still short of breath all the time, but my kitties soothed my pain. They eagerly greeted me at the door when I came home from work. They snuggled with me constantly. That winter I spent a lot of my time writing, and my kitties would sit next to me purring as I wrote. They became my best friends.

Wednesday, December 15, 2010
Dear Diary,

This morning I spent time with my kitties. Their cuteness is overwhelming. Their tiny pink noses are pure bliss. Their licks tickle me from the inside out and I feel alive around them. I feel connected to them. Without any words they simply understand me and my process. They truly love me and are teaching me how to love myself unconditionally. After a morning with them I drove into Ashland. I saw birds in huge groupings above my car, they were circling high above me in the sky; they brought me a sense of ease, which I am desperate to feel. I wish so badly that this lung illness would come to a completion. Why me? I ponder. What next? How do I continue like this? The answer came to me as I was watching the birds soar: through unconditionally loving myself. Through seeing my beauty in every moment. Through seeing my grace, my gentleness, my ease. What I need more of is love, for my condition, my situation, my broken lung. It is a journey walking through this illness. I am reminded of my inner strength when I read my Patagonia journal passages, and I remember that I can do this. If I can climb mountains,

I can devote my life to loving myself. I can do this as challenging as it seems at times. The external world seems to shout messages saying "you are not good enough the way you are," but I need to continually remind myself of my inner light, and remind myself I am magnificent just as I am. Just as I am right now. I am love! I can unconditionally love myself if I can climb mountains. I can learn to love my condition, my weakened state. I am LOVE! A thought comes to mind: **BORN TO LOVE,** *and as I write this a bird soars by my window.*

One day while Moe was lying on my chest purring, I was working on my computer and came across something I had written before my illness. It sparked my heart.

> *As my feet pound across the muddy trails and my hands move swiftly through the cold morning air, I feel grateful to be alive and running. Each morning I awake to the same beeping; I role out of bed, put on my old t-shirt with holes in it, tie the laces of my dirt covered running shoes, and head straight for the trails. My heart beats to the rhythm of the land as my body becomes one with the motions.*

As I reviewed what I had written, I was reminded of my dedication to running. I spent ten years fully dedicated to running every morning. I was known as a runner, and it was my identity. My life revolved around running. I ran in college and on running teams after college; I ran at 5 o'clock in the morning and in the midst of winter. I was truly committed to running. When I became ill I was no longer able to run and I had to let go of it. My heart was calling me to pursue a new path. I heard the call and became dedicated with my whole being, more than I had been to running.

As I open like the radiant sunlight, dwell in my eternal light, and practice the power of love, I begin to expand my horizons and I can truly breathe. As I unconditionally love all that is, I am reminded of what is real and that only love truly exists.

Chapter 6

The Magnificence of a Pure Inner Being

December 23, 2010
Dear Diary,

As I drove through the fog up the mountain road, I felt pain in my left lower lung. I wanted to be able to breathe and relax more than anything, but I could not take a full breath. I called on the light within; I asked it to shine on areas that needed healing. I imagined light filling my lungs and began to cry. When I reached the top of the forested mountain road, I saw a huge circle shining brightly – it was a brilliant beauty, it was stunning. Behind the fog was the sun. At that moment I became aware of the power, the beauty, the magnificence of the light within me, and I knew with this bright light anything was possible.

It was during December that I became aware of the full radiance of the light within my heart, but it was not until four years later that I was fully grounded in my light. Late in February 2011 my health took a turn downward. I became extremely thin and ill. I was on the brink of life. My lung pain had worsened and my shortness of breath was unbearable. I met a man who was interested in me, which triggered my anxiety and anorexia further. He was charming, flirtatious, and handsome. He made me feel good, a feeling for which I had been starving. When he would not call, my fear of abandonment was triggered and my anxiety heightened. I began having panic attacks at work. The doctors were not sure what to do with me because they were unaware that I was suffering with anorexia. A part of me knew I was restricting my food intake, and I was terrified to gain weight, but I was still in denial. It was like I was in a room with one shade open and one shade closed. I could see the spiritual world, but I did not fully understand the depth of my anorexia, and I did not know how to let go of my fears. My body was in a constant state of anxiety. I prayed and prayed. I called Dr. Katherine, and she said something that hit home: "Think of your body as the little girl within you that needs more love and nourishment. Allow your body plenty of what it needs, and as you nourish yourself think of nourishing and loving your little girl who was ostracized growing up. Read books on self-care." I bought the books *The Art of Extreme Self-Care* by Cheryl Richardson and *Self-Nurture* by Alice D. Domar, Ph. D. and Henry Dreher. These books changed my life.

April 4, 2011
Dear Diary,

I just finished reading the book, The Art of Extreme Self-Care, *and I want extreme self-care, self-nurture, and self-love. So I am answering important questions in my life and drawing from my responses.* What's most important to me at this time? *Healing my lungs, aligning with my heart, and healing my inner child.* If I could do anything I wanted without restrictions, what would it be? *To BREATHE and be able to move my body, swim, run, PLAY, hike, jump, and be in NATURE. Be in a co-creative, playful, nurturing relationship based on pure UNCONDITIONAL LOVE. Not work in the hospital, but in my healing space.* Where would I like to spend more of my time? *In nature, receiving massages, and in warm baths.* Are there areas of my life that need my attention? *YES, my physical health, nurturing it, keeping it warm, and healing my physical body.* What needs less attention? *My weight. Worrying about my weight.* Is there a secret dream or desire that is always put on hold that I'd like to devote more time to? *Getting up early to be in a really special spot in nature and meditate there. Doing gentle yoga.*

Seven days later I experienced a true miracle. On April 8, 2011, I was working at the hospital. I don't know how I was physically able to do that looking back, but I tolerated it. I had learned to tolerate extreme discomfort and pain in my daily life. I was feeling extremely short of breath as a co-worker began talking to me. She told me of a time in her life when she felt she could not go on. She turned to God and said, "I give it to you, I surrender." The next day her life completely changed. This conversation stayed with me all day and all night.

April 9, 2011
Dear Diary,

I felt a wave come crashing over my whole body, a wave of constriction, a wave of fear and judgment, and my lungs took the brunt of it. I could not breathe. I was at work in the midst of a demanding twelve-hour shift, running from room to room. I called the supervisor and told her I just had an asthma attack and could not breathe. Luckily, I was able to make it home safely. I tried everything I had access to: inhalers, teas, and vitamins. Nothing seemed to work. In a panic I called my brother. "I cannot breathe, what should I do? My inhalers are not helping, please help me!" My brother advised me to go into my body and allow my body to do what it naturally does, heal. I could barely make it in the door without collapsing. I greeted my two cats, and their affection and warmth soothed my pain. It took everything I had to make it up the stairs onto my healing table. I put one hand on my heart and one on my belly and then I called on my light within for healing. I told myself that if I awake in the morning then I know I am here for a higher purpose. I said I cannot do this any longer, universe show me the way to health. I need help and lots of it. I am here to be healthy.

The next morning, my life began to take a radical turn, one that I did not see coming. I awoke knowing that I was alive for a purpose greater than me. During morning meditation, I asked my angels for help. I imagined immense light coming to me and surrounding me. That morning I cried and said, "Spirit, I surrender. I give it you. Please show me the way back to my breath." I imagined countless beings of light coming to help me heal. Then, as if on cue, a policeman knocked on my door. My brother had called him, worried about me. I told the officer I was okay and that I had turned off my phone which explained why my brother could not reach me. After the officer left, I called my brother and told him I was spending the day at home resting. My brother was very concerned; despite our past, he still cared for me deeply. I told him I was going to be okay as I knew deep inside that I would be. I awoke in the morning still alive, and I knew I was on the earth for a higher purpose beyond this body.

That day I happened upon a business card given to me by an acquaintance one week prior. It was for a massage therapist and healer named Linda. The card boasted "Healthy Transformations," and as I read this, my heart began radiating sensations of warmth and love. I called Linda that day, and that night she was in my healing space. When she began massaging me and sending me Reiki healing energy, my whole body became extremely hot and I sweated profusely. She told me I had no "chi" in my legs and the pneumonia had almost taken my life. I knew at that point I was near death. She had the intuition to give me osha root for my lungs and stomach. As a result of my anorexia, my stomach was in pain constantly, and I was very constipated. Osha root helps to stimulate appetite and digestion, and it is very healing for the lungs and stomach. I drank cup after cup of osha root that night, took a warm bath with Epsom salts and went to bed. The next day Linda came over again. I was very weak, and it was a challenge for me to walk up the stairs. As we went into my healing room, Linda said she saw green healing energy coming out of my hands. They were heating up; I put them on myself. Linda began massaging my neck and sending me an abundance of Reiki healing energy. Within ten minutes I had to sit up. I began coughing up large amounts of blood and mucous from my lungs. During one cough I felt a chunk expel from my left lower lobe. After that treatment, I could fully breathe into my left lung like I had never done before. Linda said, "You are releasing all the fear and judgments you have been swallowing, and the asthma and pneumonia you have been carrying in your lungs are expelling."

With the little physical strength I had left, I used my whole spirit to stand and loudly exclaim, "I will no longer swallow others' judgments! I am reclaiming my health and my life!" I expelled more blood and mucous. I was coughing and crying, repeatedly. I was releasing enormous amounts of energy in the form of blood and mucous. I said again, "I am reclaiming my health!" After expelling two gallons of blood and fluid from my lungs, I sat on the edge of my healing table and had the most profound moment of my life. I felt the presence of divine unconditional love wash over me. The presence was crystal clear, gentle, graceful, radiant, and the most loving feeling I had ever experienced. The presence radiated from within and all around me. The presence was enormous. My angels were all around me. It was an extraordinary miracle. I felt true unconditional love. I felt the presence of Spirit, the Light, and all that is. I began crying with tears of love and compassion for myself and what I had been through. I felt pure unconditional love. I had come to know that unconditional love is what we are made of and what ultimately heals us. From that moment on I was truly dedicated to loving myself unconditionally.

Linda told me she saw an energetic cord from my childhood that was wrapped around my neck and had come off in the healing session. Old, stuck energy had left my body, she said. She told me I had an extremely beautiful soul. I began crying. Rarely was I seen as having a soul. I was always seen as tall, as an object. With courage and strength I said, "I will not swallow fear any longer. I will not allow judgments to take over my body. I am reclaiming my birthright of health." I coughed up more blood and mucous. Linda gave me healing water to drink, Mt. Shasta water that was infused with Reiki energy. I was having a hard time swallowing from all the coughing and releasing of stuck energy, chronic pneumonia, and severe asthma. It was hard to even swallow water. That night I awoke and vomited and coughed up more blood. I said, "Fear, you are not allowed here." With strength and conviction I raised my arms in the air and said, "Fear, you do not belong here. Get out of my body! I am saving my body, which encompasses a very loving, bright soul." I gathered all the strength, courage and fire within my being to save my life. I was determined to reclaim my birthright of bliss and radiant health, and I was not going to allow fear to take over my life any longer. I saw huge waves of light encircle me; I cried and coughed up more blood. With courage and determination I loudly told the universe, "I am reclaiming my birthright of radiant health!"

The next morning Linda came over again. I was drinking osha root tea and healing water and still coughing up blood. Linda told me I was releasing and cleansing. She told me that I was coughing out the pneumonia and asthma. I talked to her about my past, my struggles with anorexia, my struggles with my family, my lung illness, my healing gifts, my running, and I was crying and coughing up blood throughout my story. Linda told me to take a deep breath in and reassure my body that I was there for it now. Then, I put one hand on my heart and one hand on my stomach, and I told my body I was so sorry for starving it and I was going to do my best to nurture it from this point forward. I asked my body to forgive me, and it did. I made a contract with my body to love and nurture it to the very best of my abilities. I felt a real and deep connection to my body. I felt compassion and love towards my body. And from that point forward I was truly dedicated to nurturing and loving my body the best I could.

Linda gave me a book called, *The Essene Gospel of Peace* from The Third Century Aramaic Manuscript and Old Slavonic Texts compared, edited, and translated by Edmond Bordeaux Szekely. I opened the book and read.

> For the power of God's angels enters into you with the living food which the Lord gives you from his royal table. And when you eat, have above you the angel of air, and below you the angel of water. Breathe long and deeply at all your meals, and the angel of air will bless you. And chew well your food with your teeth, that it become water, and that the angel of water turn it into blood in your body. And eat slowly, as it were a prayer you make to God. For I tell you truly, the power of God enters into you when you eat in this manner.

Later that afternoon I was sitting at my round glass kitchen table and I felt the presence of Spirit. I stood up and felt white energy circling the table. I held hands with my angels as we circled the table, and I asked them to help me love and nourish my body. I asked for healing around food and nourishment.

My body had become so thin and weak that I was extremely cold most of the time, and after coughing up so much blood I was having difficulty swallowing. Linda received the intuitive message to make me Miso soup with root veggies (beets, carrots, sweet potatoes, and parsnips) and lemon balm tea. I loved the Miso soup; it was warm and nourishing to my very weak physical state. I pureed the soup to make it easier to swallow. I imagined white light and angels going into my body as I ate the healing Miso soup. It was the first time I felt real nourishment. I felt angels enter into me with the living Miso soup.

Linda also had the intuition to use lavender and eucalyptus essential oils. She rubbed the eucalyptus on my back and where my left lung resides. I used the lavender to calm my nervous system. I inhaled it, put it in my bath, and rubbed it all over my skin. The lavender was comforting for my deteriorated state. It wouldn't be until years later that I would fully understand the magic and power of essential oils. They are not only gifts from the earth, but energetic properties that hold high vibrations. The lavender and eucalyptus were staples in my daily healing regimen from that point forward.

That week I expelled buckets of energy, but it would take me several years to truly integrate a new way of being into my life. I released old energy, but I had to learn how to bring the light into my physical state, heal my body, change my daily thought patterns about food and body image, learn assertiveness, gain the confidence to talk about my spiritual experiences, and fully become my soul walking on the planet. This was a process of inner work that took time. Energy can shift over night, but learning a new way to be in the world takes patience, commitment, and perseverance. The Reiki healing I received provided me with the ability to fully commit to nourishing and loving my body and learning to live in a new way.

I could not talk to my family yet; how would they understand what had just happened? I stayed at home with my cats doing everything I could to help me with this process: drinking healing water, osha root and lemon balm tea, receiving healings from Linda, eating Miso soup, rubbing lavender and eucalyptus on my skin, reading *The Essene Gospel of Peace*, coughing up blood, taking warm Epsom salt baths, wrapping myself in warm blankets, praying, crying, and writing. I could barely walk up the stairs, but I wrote in my journal daily.

April 10, 2011 – 9:00 am

I see the Light. I appreciate the crystal light all around me. I am truly dedicated to divine love. I am dedicated to my cultivation of the light. I am magical and supernatural. Anything that does not originate from the heart is an illusion. This too shall pass. There are so many good things waiting for me. I am on the cusp of exploding in love.

April 10, 2011 – 12:00 pm

I deserve happiness, I deserve respect, I deserve love, I appreciate my being: gentle, sweet, brilliant, beautiful, amazing, radiant, serene, and colorful. I am a goddess, and I am transforming into crystalline energy. I have nothing to fear, this too shall pass. I am becoming stronger day by day. I am a child of the universe. I am a pure crystal energy. I am here to awaken to bliss. I AM LOVE. I am going to make the best of where I am. I deserve respect and unconditional love. I deserve the fruits of life.

April 10, 2011 – 2:00 pm

I am grateful for my connection with nature and the animals. Goals: to write a book, to have my own healing practice, to feel confident in my body.

My lungs are my teacher. I am transforming every day. I am opening like a radiant sun, dwelling in eternal light. I am expanding my wings.

I am committed to light and love. I am on an unfolding journey. There is nothing to fear. I am growing each day. I am on a healing journey opening up to new horizons and new opportunities. Truly, there is nothing to fear. I am brave. I am letting go, and I forgive myself. My lungs are beautiful. I am love and I am expanding in love. I do not have to be perfect, I can be me. There is nothing by which to be judged or of which to be ashamed. I can let go of self-judgment and perfectionism. My highself loves me unconditionally, unconditionally. I am walking home.

April 10, 2011 – 6:00 pm

I am a midwife of the new humanity. I am divine. This is my divine path. Self-love is about seeing myself as a divine human. Love is forever expanding, unfolding, creating, and illuminating. I am a miracle. I am committed to unconditional, non-judgmental, gentle, real love. I am pouring love out through my heart.

April 11, 2011

Who am I? I am the Light. I am peace. I am love. I am this enormous golden light. This anxiety is not really me. I can let go of this now. I can let go of the illusion of right and wrong. I allow this anxiety, this entity, to go into the golden ray of light. I release you now. I am not you, you no longer serve me, you no longer belong here. I am love and light, a ray of golden sunshine, you may go now and leave, you have served your purpose. You no longer serve me or my work here. This dark anxious force may leave my soul now. Please leave my body. I release all negative emotions, toxicities, and anxieties to the light, and I come home to my eternal light. I am a golden ray of healing light. I release all toxic emotions, negative beliefs, and illusions. I am a golden light of grace. I want to stay here and experience my light. I have made it this far, I can stay and experience bliss. We are born to make manifest the Glory of God within us. I want to stay here and experience all the universe has to offer me. I have compassion for myself and all beings. My true state is one of peace, serenity, love, and light. I release all fears to the universe to be recycled. I allow my golden light to shine.

April 12, 2011

I am awakening my true potential. I am aligning with my birthright, bliss. I am aligning with my true potential in all areas of my life, body, mind, and spirit. I am standing tall. Well-being is my birthright. I am aligning with my birthright to be healthy. What I am going through is not my fault. I release all fears and anything that does not serve my higher purpose. I reclaim my sacred spirit.

April 14, 2011, evening

I call on my angel within. She is here to support me and to guide me to unconditional love. I reclaim my divine birthright of perfect health. I let go of all toxic thoughts. I am getting stronger every day in mind, body, and spirit. My birthright is bliss. I reclaim my birthright of harmony and divine health. I call on the healing, golden light to assist me. I call upon all my angels. I am reclaiming my health and my life. I follow the divine guidance of my body, intuition, and spirit. I am here to be in radiant health. I am here to play. I am peace. I am strong. I am gentle. I am here to be radically healthy. I call on my angel within. It is pointless to resist life's natural flow. I accept my body's divine timing.

April 15, 2011

Spirit is sacred and pulling me through. I am strong like the mountains. I am embracing my inner child. I am coming home to my intuition and opening up to my highself.

April 16, 2011

I am getting stronger every day in mind, body, and spirit. I am the Light. I am here to heal. I am healing right now. Yes, I can run again. Yes, I can be free. Yes, I can create well-being. Yes, I can nurture my body back to health. I am reclaiming my birthright of freedom and radiant health. I am transforming into unconditional love. I allow myself to be me.

As I allow my wounds to heal, step into my radiant light,
feel my own expansion, and dance to my own drum beat,
I see the light in all others as clearly as I see my own.

CHAPTER 7

Free Falling

On April 16, 2011, a cold, spring day, I was sitting at the edge of my kitchen table wearing purple fleece pants and holding a glass jar filled with blood and mucous. Two familiar faces appeared at my front door. My heart skipped a beat when I saw my parents standing in front of my home unexpectedly. I thought, how would they understand the depth of transforming happening within my inner being? They were going to be stunned about how sick and thin I had become. I did not have the energy to explain myself. My mother had been concerned about my anorexia for years.

I opened the door. My parents erupted into tears when they saw how thin and ill I appeared. I was pale, skin and bones, and coughing up blood into a glass jar. My father was sobbing, peeled over on the ground. He expressed emotions for me I had never seen before. He said, "Not my Ali. No, not her too." My family had a history of addictions and he did not want to see me struggling with anorexia. They immediately wanted to take me back home to Minnesota. I said with courage and anger, "I just had a transformation in my healing room. An energetic cord was removed from my neck. I will not swallow fear and judgments from the family any longer. I don't want to go to your home in Minnesota where there is so much judgment and fear. I can heal here." My parents continued sobbing. They were truly frightened. They stayed with me through that evening and night.

The next day my parents tried to convince me again to come home with them. I continued to refuse. I was afraid that if I went with them that the energetic cord would again wrap around my neck. That evening they asked me to talk with Patrick, my brother's therapist. I trusted Patrick because I had previously read parts of his book and knew he could see energy. I agreed to talk to Patrick on the phone. I told him I did not want to go back to Minnesota because I did not want the energetic cord to wrap around my being after I had just expelled it. He said, "You are very ill. Your body is very weak and you need the physical support from your parents right now. They may not understand your spiritual awakening process, but they can help you gain your physical health back. Take their physical support. The energetic cord is now gone, and it will never come back. You have nothing to fear. You will have a beautiful life, but first get your physical strength back." I trusted his words. After that conversation I went inward and asked my heart if it was best for me to go back to Minnesota with my parents. My heart said yes.

I told my parents I was coming home with them and they started smiling and crying. They said, "We can all leave tomorrow, but first we want you to go to the hospital to get an exam and a chest x-ray." I agreed. In the hospital I received IV fluids which helped my body gain some strength and a chest x-ray which revealed that my lungs were clear.

Leaving my home in Ashland, Oregon felt like free falling out of an airplane without knowing if my landing would be soft. I truly had to let go and allow a power greater than myself to take over. Deep down I knew this was the best thing for me, but it was terrifying. I was incredibly weak and I needed physical support and family around me to gain my strength. My inner and spiritual focus had become very strong over the past year, and now it was time to integrate the physical reality back into my life and fully heal my body. I truly had to surrender, forgive myself for what had happened, and allow others to help.

I had one day to gather a bag of belongings before flying back to Minneapolis, my childhood home. I packed my book *The Essene Gospel of Peace,* my white angelic bowl from Dena, my lavender and eucalyptus essential oils, my journal, my computer, a small angel figurine freely spreading her arms holding two birds, and a few clothing items. I also brought my two cats with me on the plane. They sat on my lap in cat carriers, and we comforted each other. I left everything else behind including my sky blue convertible beetle. The hardest items to leave behind were my paintings because they were irreplaceable and very close to my heart. I did not know if I would get my belongings back, but I surrendered. I let go of what I no longer needed in more ways than one. And what filled my life in the upcoming years was one hundred fold.

As we drove to the airport, I was very anxious. I was still coughing up blood, my stomach hurt, it was still hard to swallow, and I was extremely weak. I was worried how I was physically going to make it on the plane. I was concerned about being back in Minneapolis, and living with my parents. I had no idea of what was to come. I could not make my healing Miso soup and drink osha root tea on the plane. I was terrified about my physical state. I allowed my angels to take over. I did not have the time or strength to say goodbye to anyone in Ashland including Dena. She did not even know I was leaving. I left Ashland that cold April day close to death, the sickest I had been in my whole life, and I returned three years later with a strong, vibrant, renewed body, the healthiest I had ever been.

When I arrived at my childhood home, I felt uprooted and disoriented. I had not been in a big city in four years, and I had just come out of being alone in my home for five days where I went through the most profound, transformative energy healing of my life. The big buildings, the crowds of people, and the noises were jarring to my sensitive system. I felt like it was the first time I had ever seen Minneapolis. I felt reborn. That first week I spent most of my time in my parents' home resting, meditating, drinking tea, and eating warming foods. I slowly integrated solid foods back into my system. After being in starvation for months, it was important for me to slowly reintroduce foods into my body. Slowly I learned to nourish myself. I was still terrified to gain weight, but I was dedicated to loving and nurturing myself. I talked to Linda the first week back at my parents' home, and she helped me choose nourishing foods for my body. She also helped me with my relationship with my parents. She told me I was in the process of reclaiming my life and health, and it was important for me to assert my physical and emotional needs and tell my parents how I was feeling. When I felt judged by my parents, I started to speak my truth. I did not want to swallow their judgments and fear any longer. It was time for me to assert my right to be alive and healthy.

Linda sent me a book in the mail called *You Can Heal Your Life* by Louise Hay. This book became very close to my heart. It reinforced what I learned from Dr. Katherine: the importance of loving thoughts and self-love. I continued to write in my self-love journal daily and practice loving affirmations. I learned that part of transforming into my soul was aligning my thoughts with those of my soul. Loving thoughts were in alignment with my soul, and judgmental thoughts were not. I was becoming more aware of my inner dialogue. When judgmental thoughts would surface I would realign my thinking with my heart. I started saying daily, "I love and approve of myself," and eventually I started feeling unconditional love for myself. I was planting seeds in my mind that one day manifested in my life. In childhood I was trained to think critically and judgmentally, therefore it took me years to change my thought patterns into loving messages. I have learned that most of our thoughts are subconscious, and it can take years to peel away the subconscious layers. That year I started becoming aware of my subconscious thoughts and learned the importance of daily loving affirmations. My mind was aligning with my heart.

The willow tree on my parents' property was very grounding for me. I would spend hours sitting under it journaling and talking with my angels. I spent every morning looking out my childhood bedroom window into the majestic nature all around me and asking my angels for assistance with healing. The nature on my parents' property gave me support and unconditional love during that abrupt transition.

One night during my first week home, my mom sat on the living room couch with me and told me about a healing program that could help me. She said there were support groups, weekly acupuncture, massages, and that the program helped women who struggled with body image. It all sounded great until we looked it up online and I saw that it was a program for women with eating disorders. Instantly

I started sobbing. I was so sad that I had struggled with anorexia. I was terrified to go to treatment for it because I had heard that treatment centers make you eat fast food at every meal. I was very afraid to eat any "bad foods" thinking they would harm me, lower my vibration, cause enormous weight gain, and prolong my healing process. I wanted to nourish my body through organic root veggies, Miso soup, organic whole grains, and foods of my own choice. But to receive the help that I needed, I had to let go of control completely and surrender. I was scared that the people at the treatment center would not understand my spirituality. I questioned whether they would understand what I had been through. Would they understand the depth of my energy healing treatment with Linda? Would they understand my spiritual awakening process? Would they understand, accept, or love me?

Saturday, May 1, 2011
Dear Diary,

I am back in Minnesota in my childhood home. My mom is trying to send me to an eating disorder treatment center, but I want to eat real nourishing whole foods to heal my body back to radiant health. I have heard that eating disorder treatment centers feed you fast food. One part of me says this is my opportunity to stand up for me, to say this is what I want and this is what I believe, and I want to heal through living food, not fast food. And the other part of me says go and enjoy, eat the different foods and learn that it isn't what we eat but how we eat it: with love and compassion for ourselves. Learn to eat without food judgments. I am at a fork in the road and I do not know which direction to go. Angels, please help.

After much inner work, I surrendered to help. I needed the help of The Emily Program to fully regain my strength, and I could not do it on my own. I accepted my mom's request to go to the treatment program with hesitancy and fear.

During the first week back at my parents' home, I was still very weak and anxious. It took all the courage and strength I had to just walk to the mailbox. I was terrified to move my body again, worried that my lungs would relapse. Even though I coughed out all the pneumonia and asthma, the lung pain and shortness of breath I experienced was still vivid in my mind, and I was terrified to re-experience it. I took baby steps each day. After walking to the mailbox, my goal was to walk around the neighborhood block. I was excited, yet terrified to move my body again.

Monday, May 3, 2011
Dear Diary,

The sun is shining brightly into the eastern hemisphere of my childhood home. As I sit cross-legged in the beautiful living room listening to my favorite music and watching the sun rise, I feel that my journey has taken on a new chapter. I feel scared, excited, and unsure of what the future may hold. For now, I know I must be patient and embrace my new chapter with warm, open arms.

Tuesday, May 4, 2011
Dear Diary,

I am reflecting on my life. I was a magical child. One who loved animals especially horses. One who loved nature, imaginary play, and arts and crafts. I spent my childhood days playing on the swing set, building forts in the forest, pretending I was flying all over the world, painting collages, and playing vet with all the animals of the household. I was soft, sensitive, and gentle. I was a peacemaker. I was in tune with nature, animals, and the spirit world. I was not your average child and my peers, teachers, and family tried to shape and limit me to stay within societal norms. In turn, I felt restricted, suffocated, and isolated.

I was bullied in school, sports, at the stable, and home. My father was emotionally absent or loud with anger, my mother was highly critical, and my brother told me I was a gross giant who would never have a boyfriend. I grew unusually fast, and I was bullied and shunned at school every day for being too tall, too sensitive, and too original. My older brother was popular and everyone loved him. My parents put him on a pedestal and me in the dirt. My parents were not aware of the torture going on between my brother and I, and I protected him. I did not feel safe to be me, and I did not feel safe in my body.

Flash forward to April 2014: It took me years to unravel the trauma of my childhood and assert my right to be alive on Earth. But I did. I healed and recovered, and I now know healing is possible for all beings. Hope prevails in my heart for all children, all families, all animals, all living things, and all of humanity.

Horses, nature, and the running trails were my love and my safe haven. I started riding horses at the age of eight. The horses loved me unconditionally and so did nature. I moved out west for college to be closer to the mountains, to nature. After nursing school, I moved to a small mountain town, Ashland, Oregon, and not only fell in love with the beautiful mountains and trails all around me, but with my first boyfriend. He was tall, blonde, and blue-eyed, and he truly thought I was beautiful. It was the first time I felt adored. He also had a love for nature and animals. We spent our days hiking and backpacking.

We were in nature as much as possible. I became immersed in his family and small town community. We spent as much time together as our schedules would allow. But as time went on, I realized that in order for me to completely heal from my childhood wounds I would need to leave him. He also had childhood wounds, and we had bonded over this common ground. I set out on a journey trying to end the relationship; it was the most challenging task I had encountered yet.

My creative and artistic side was stifled in the relationship with him. In a sense I lost myself within that relationship. I so badly wanted to be adored and loved by a man that I gave up a part of myself for it. After ending that relationship, my spiritual connection became stronger. I was chanting and meditating every morning. I began the process of finding my creative side again, as well as my sensitivity. I had shoved my sensitivity into a deep, dark corner within and masked it with muscles from running. My sensitivity was shunned growing up, and I had not yet learned how to love it and allow it to shine through. I have come to learn that my sensitivity is one of my most beautiful qualities; it is similar to butterfly wings. Their wings are sensitive and fragile, yet stunning and mystical. After ending the destructive relationship, I began the process of digging deep down within my soul to allow it to blossom one day. Just as is needed for a beautiful flower to fully blossom, the soil must be dug up and churned first.

Today I feel I am on the path of becoming free. Loving myself and following my heart no matter what anyone says or thinks of me. That is true freedom.

Within two weeks, I had a spot in The Emily Program which is highly unusual as most people have to wait three to six months to get into the program. It truly was divine intervention. It was the beginning of May, and I drove myself in my convertible to the program center. My father and brother had flown to Oregon the week before to retrieve my belongings and drive my car home. It was my first time driving again since the beginning of April. It felt good to be in my convertible and listen to music. I loved driving with the top down; I felt so close to nature and free. When I arrived at the center, I was anxious about being judged for being thin, weird, having body image difficulties, or being the odd one out. I was terrified no one would understand my spiritual awakening process. Once I opened the door, I saw other women who were struggling with the same things. I checked in and waited to speak to a therapist. A gentle woman called my name and I followed her back. I explained my struggles during childhood, my addiction to running, my fear of bad foods, and my lung illness. She listened with compassion. I felt relieved that I wasn't being judged. Following my meeting with the therapist, I met with a nutritionist. She was very laid back and artsy. She had a picture of a butterfly hanging on her wall that said "one day the caterpillar will transform into a butterfly." I instantly felt safe with her. She reassured me that we would not be eating hamburgers at every meal, which was an initial fear of mine. She also explained the meal plan at The Emily Program and that I would start on a restorative plan to work towards a healthy weight. I would then begin a meal plan designed to maintain a healthy weight. I was scared, but I was committed to my body and my health. From that day forward, I followed my meal plan, and I have never turned back.

Saturday, May 14, 2011
Dear Diary,

It feels like there is actually a hole inside me, I feel empty. I know in my mind I need to love myself, and I know that happiness comes from within. But how do I FEEL this love and bliss from within? I have a roof over my head and food in front of me, the cutest kitties in the world, a beautiful car, and clothes to wear, but I feel empty inside emotionally. I feel a void. I have tried to fill this void with running and an eating disorder. I said goodbye to running a year ago, and I am in the midst of saying goodbye to this eating disorder voice. I could switch my addiction to shopping or shoes or beauty products, but I would rather fill this void inside with inner LOVE. How does one find inner peace, inner love within? TRUE freedom.

Sunday, May 15, 2011
Dear Diary,

I was driving along with the top of my convertible down. I saw the birds fly, I saw light behind the clouds, and I felt connected to all that is. I felt whole, safe, peaceful, and loved. The void within me was gone; it had vanished. I felt truly connected. I want to know how to feel like this most of the time, to feel whole, complete, and connected in my daily life. I want to feel in love with life, in love with myself, and feel alive from within. Right now I feel connected and loved 20% of the time and 80% of the time I feel an empty, lonely void within. I want to switch that, change the channel, feel in tune and positive about life and alive 80% of the time, and 20% of the time feel a bit off. How can I flip the switch regardless of external circumstance, regardless of my physical state, regardless of my parents' beliefs, regardless of others around me and external matters? I want to feel whole within.

Monday, May 16, 2011
Dear Diary,

The Emily Program starts soon. I am frightened to speak my truth and navigate the waters of change. Mostly I am frightened that the people at the treatment center will not accept me. My desires, my wants, my wishes, and my dreams have always been seen as unrealistic and different. I have always been told my thoughts are too idealistic, irrational, out there, just "wishful thinking," and unrealistic. I have always been given the message that I am too much and that my dreams will not come true. I have never felt completely safe and embraced by humans. I have only felt accepted and loved by nature and animals. I am scared to not be accepted at the program.

My anorexia has been a manifestation of wanting to be loved by the human world. Now I need to learn to love myself within and not allow the human world to affect my internal world so much. My anorexic lifestyle began seven years ago, and now I am learning a new way of being. My anorexia began in college; I was known as the strong Amazon woman. I was on the crew team and spent three months mountaineering and kayaking in Chile, Patagonia. I was stronger than most of the mountain men there. I was a powerful mountain woman and was mocked for it. My sensitive, gentle soul swallowed the rude judgments. As a result of the increased emotional stress, my cycle became irregular and I went to the doctor. She diagnosed me with polycystic ovary syndrome and told me to watch my caloric intake and my sugar levels. I was terrified. I read every book within reach that discussed health, whole foods, or nutritional healing. I went on a detox diet and switched from crew to my preferred form of movement, running. I became a solid member of the track and field team. Upon arriving home for summer break, my mom panicked. "WOW, you're too thin," she said. "You must see a nutritionist." Yes, I had lost weight, and although I knew my mother's concern was well-intended, her method of expressing that concern stung deeply and left me feeling criticized by my mother. The comments about my weight felt like harsh judgments, just as the rude remarks about being an "Amazon woman" felt downright awful. No matter what shape or size my body was, it would never be good enough to the outside world, and internally I struggled. I felt unlovable. I went to see a nutritionist that summer, but she talked mostly about calories. While this was generally informative, it did not help with my anorexic mindset. I remained a runner. I ate all organic, avoided dairy due to my childhood asthma, and restricted my food intake.

Monday, May 16, 2011
Dear Diary,

The universe is bringing me what I need to move to the next level of self-actualization. Everything is a mirror for my further growth. So as I trust the universe, I learn to trust the messages of my body and my inner being!

Tuesday, May 17, 2011
Dear Diary,

I went to a massage appointment today. I walked up the stairs of the Minneapolis home and stepped into the healing room. It brought back memories of my healing room in Ashland. My healing room was a very unique and special room. The energy in it was magical, and I missed it.

The massage therapist asked me how I was feeling. I told her I was working through self-love and self-nourishment. During the massage, I was thinking of my Ashland healing room and Linda. I missed Linda. This massage room was too cold for me to fully enjoy the experience, and I did not feel safe with the therapist like I had with Linda. I longed for a new, wonderful massage therapist. I built up the courage to ask her to turn the heat up, and as it got warmer, I started feeling better.

While on the table I revealed to the massage therapist that I was going to an eating disorder treatment center soon, and I was terrified because I wanted to only eat organic pure foods. The massage therapist said I should not go to the treatment center and I should eat what I want. This provoked a lot of anxiety within me because I am terrified to eat "bad foods." I am worried non-organic, non-pure foods filled with toxins and chemicals will hurt my lungs, lower my vibration, cause enormous weight gain, and cause constipation.

Wednesday, May 18, 2011
Dear Diary,

I am learning to allow myself to be where I am on my path of having unconditional love for myself and complete self-acceptance. I am learning to ask what I need for the goodness of my physical and emotional beings. I am learning self-nourishment, more than just for my physical state, but my whole being. I want to BE FREE. Free of restrictive thought patterns. Free of worry about external measures. Free of anxiety and worry about my lung illness returning. I am learning that freedom is about trusting and about following the guidance of the soul. The eating disorder voice is fear, the conditioned mind is fear, but that is not me. That is not my soul. When I listen to my soul and my heart and trust my light within, I feel empowered.

The universe is guiding me on the path to becoming free, which means freedom anywhere, at The Emily Program, with any plate of food in front of me, or around people who judge me. I am learning to stand up for my body, stand up for my needs, express myself, and nurture my inner child.

Unconditional love, heart energy, is the most powerful energy in the universe, and it can overcome anything. I will send love to the food I eat, and therefore my body will take in the love and nourishment. I will accept what is on my plate. I will accept what life brings me. I will learn to accept myself. I am learning to follow my heart and divine path. I am learning in each moment to flow with grace. I will do my best.

There is only this moment, sensing and feeling what the body needs in this moment and what the spirit and heart are calling for. I allow my heart to speak.

The next day I met a living angel. She was a physician's assistant at The Emily Program. When I was on her table having my vital signs checked, she asked about my work. I became emotional talking about my previous nursing job. I told her how stressed I had been, and how that job was not in alignment with my heart. She understood and helped me to process why I had chosen that career field. I had sought out nursing because my mom wanted me to, not because it was in alignment with who I was. Before I went into nursing, I wanted to be a midwife. My heart was called towards natural healing. My mother told me it was important to receive western medical training before I pursued natural healing. I wanted her approval so I went into nursing first. Today, I practice integrative healing. I am a yoga teacher, Reiki Master, and Reiki hospice nurse. I am a spiritual midwife, here to help with the birthing of a divine human race.

I also shared with the physician's assistant how I had been allowed only thirty minutes to eat at work during a twelve-hour shift, and because of that I developed severe anxiety related to eating at work. I always felt extremely rushed and did not know if I was going to be able to finish my meal without interruption. When she told me that The Emily Program allotted only thirty minutes to eat as well, I was unable to hold back heavy sobs, and it was difficult to catch my breath. Since I had been home it was taking me two hours to eat as my swallow was still delayed. My body had not yet learned to trust that I would nourish it. My body was still recovering from starvation and in constant anxiety that it would not be fed adequately. In essence, eating a meal was a long process for me. I chewed my food very slowly with each bite. I did this because of what I read in *The Essene Gospel of Peace*: "And chew well your food with your teeth, that it become water, and that the angel of water turn into blood in your body. And eat slowly, as it were a prayer you make to the Lord. For I tell you truly, the power of God enters into you, if you eat after this manner at the table." I trusted these words and teachings because Linda had the intuition to give the book to me, and her intuition was powerful. I was terrified that The Emily Program was going to make me eat all kinds of foods in only thirty minutes. I thought it would be impossible. However, the physician's assistant was very reassuring and encouraging. She said if I needed, they would wait for me while I finished my meals. I was terrified to be judged about what I had gone through and the process I was still in. The physician's assistant was gentle and kind. She showed me the treatment room where I would arrive in only two short days.

May 20, 2011
Dear Diary,

There are days of accelerated awareness, feeling my being, my energy, and beginning to love myself. Then, there are days of feeling like a cloud is covering my whole being, and I cannot feel my light. I feel very low. I feel that a part of me is dying. It is almost so unbearable – to feel the pain, to feel the wound within my inner child, to feel. The days I feel truly me – my true essence – I feel bliss, I feel alive, and I want to be the best person I can be. I want to play, I want to sing, I want to eat. And I am eager for the future, eager to get well. I can hardly wait to feel my body again, to feel the dirt beneath my running shoes, and to feel the liveliness of my being. Today, self-love seems easier than yesterday. I will do my best to embrace the unfolding of my soul.

At 8 o'clock on the morning of May 21, 2011, I arrived for my first day of treatment at The Emily Program. I brought my journal, coloring pencils and pastels, osha root tea, and lavender essential oil. The treatment room had a white board, a circle of chairs, blankets, and a table where we would eat. I sat down on one of the chairs next to a side table where I could keep my colored pencils and pastels. A younger woman walked in late and sat next to me. She had the same journal as me. I instantly felt safe around her. She spoke of her troubles with self-esteem, body image, cutting, cross-country running, and swimming. I could relate to her, and her stories brought me a sense of ease. I didn't feel so alone or separated.

When I introduced myself to the group, I explained I had come from Oregon and talked about my lung illness. I did not open up about my transformative Reiki treatment, coughing up blood, or my spiritual experiences. I kept those within; they felt fragile and sacred, and I did not know how to share them or integrate them into my current reality. I was also terrified of others' judgments or disregard of my experiences.

That day I received pamphlets on eating disorders, and I also bought some books about other women's struggles with anorexia. These books helped me to identify my own anorexia. While reading them I could completely relate to the other women. I wasn't feeling so alone and isolated anymore. It was reassuring to know that others rose above the same issues. When reading these deeply personal stories, I felt compassion for the women, and therefore myself. It tore down some of the walls of shame, judgment, and secrecy I had around starving myself. These thick walls of denial and judgment I had around my anorexia were slowly being chipped away and crumbling down.

In Oregon it was easy to be in denial regarding my anorexia because no one around me knew about it or was educated on the subject. It was easy to not address my fear of food and weight gain. But in Minnesota I was forced to face these topics. Most people around me now were either experts on the treatment of eating disorders or going through the same struggles. I was terrified to gain weight. Internally, I felt huge since the days of my childhood when I was shunned for being tall. I felt big down to my bones. No matter how thin I got, I felt enormous. And in my conditioned mind, big meant ugly and unlovable. I had to face the fears of my mind and gain the weight necessary to heal my physical state. I had to heal my inner child and the perceptions of myself and the world around me to completely heal my eating disorder.

I began treatment at The Emily Program going almost daily at first, but slowly tapering off to one therapy session per week. The first week was the most challenging. I had not yet formed bonds with other clients. It was still very difficult to swallow at each meal. All the food was new to me. We ate spaghetti with meatballs. I had not eaten red meat in six years. I was unsure how my system would respond, and it was upsetting that the meat was not organic. I had cut out grains from my diet for the previous year and a half, and now I was eating white flour pasta. I had to learn to disregard the food judgments that were deeply conditioned in my mind and trust in my angels. I ate slowly and talked to my angels at each meal. I was anxious with each new meal which made it harder to swallow and breathe, but I continued on the path knowing I had a higher purpose and a deeper calling. I imagined light coming into me as I ate and remembered the circle I formed with my angels around my table in Oregon. I allowed my angels to help me. I knew nourishment was about more than just the quality of the food. It also centered on the quality of my thoughts, energy, emotions, and ultimately the presence of Spirit while I was eating. To my surprise my body tolerated all the new foods that week. I have learned that self-nourishment is about truly loving our body and nourishing our body the best we can with what we have. I needed the help of the program to restore my weight to a healthy level and maintain that weight. Today, I am able to choose what foods I eat, and I choose the most loving, nurturing foods possible for my one and only precious body. Self-nourishment is about love, not restriction and fear. I overcame my fear of certain foods at The Emily Program. There is truly nothing to fear; everything comes to us so that we may grow more in love.

May 27, 2011
Dear Diary,

I finished my first week of treatment. I love the people there. They are awesome, creative, unique, honest, heartfelt – TRUE BEINGS! The food is not my preference, and I would rather nourish my body back to health on pure organics. However, I am there for the treatment and personal connection with other people and that is more important to me at this point. I need this support system more than I need organics to nourish me back to health. I can relate to each individual there, my heart reaches out to each one. I feel at home already, and I feel safe to be me, which is a blessing. People, relationships, and finding my true self are gifts that are beginning to evolve from this life challenge. I am beginning to feel ripples of hope within my heart. The treatment center is warm and cozy. I look forward to going in the morning. I am meeting role models and new friends. I am starting to find me. When I am not wrapped up in the identity of being a runner, nurse, and salad-lover, I begin to find my inner core – my laugh, my playfulness, my creativity, my voice, and my wisdom. I am starting to find my uniqueness, my compassion, and my desire to be in a community of other creative individuals.

The wound within my heart is beginning to mend. My left lung is beginning to repair and rejuvenate moment by moment, and the void within my heart is filling with art, nature, nourishment, friends, laughter, and playfulness. Each day I learn something new about myself and my inner world, and each day I being to feel stronger in the world around me. I am learning the importance of opening up to the world and receiving the healing benefits of support and compassion. I am beginning to open to and receive LIFE. I accepted the gift of treatment.

May 28, 2011
Dear Diary,

I am sitting on the deck of my childhood home. The nature around me is pristine; the trees are strong and stable, yet still and gentle. The sky is a crisp, clear blue and the birds are chirping excitedly. The grass is green and beautifully full and fresh from the days of rain. On the swing set, I see the swing waiting for me with open arms, with a strong foundation, waiting for the moment of feeling my weight on it, feeling the weight of a real human being swinging for the pure joy of swinging – waiting for the moment of joy and freedom. I see one of my angels on the swing, and she is calling me to join her.

I see the gentle sway of the willow tree in the front yard. It is tall, strong, graceful, and extremely patient. The willow tree has been waiting for me my whole life. Waiting for me to see her – truly see her. And now I see her with an open heart and open mind.

May 29, 2011
Dear Diary,

I sat on the swing in my childhood backyard today. I could feel the presence of my angel as I sat down on the black rubber seat. She was reassuring. I was scared to swing at first, what if my lungs flared back up, I thought. My angel gave me the message that my body could handle swinging and I trusted her. Once I began moving through the air, I felt like I was flying. It was the most freedom and movement I had felt in two years. It felt mystical and magical. It reminded me of running, and I wondered when I would be able to run again, if ever. I fell in love with swinging.

After two weeks at The Emily Program I met a profound woman named Tara Cindy Sherman. It was a Monday afternoon, and I was in the yoga room at the program. The room was dimly lit, and I was lying on a pink yoga mat. Tara walked into the room and turned on soothing music. Her presence felt like home. She guided us through three-part breathing which helped me to expand my lungs and wing span. Her gentleness, soothing voice, nurturing presence, and grounding meditations were just what I needed. I was working on harmonizing my root chakra and she offered wisdom and gentle guidance. I felt completely safe around her. Now I had found a place at the program that integrated my spiritual awakening process. Recovering from an eating disorder is not only about nourishing the physical body, but also the spirit. Yoga has been a profound source of spiritual nourishment for me.

After yoga class I approached Tara to thank her. It felt like we had known each other for years. Her bright blue eyes were familiar to me. I asked her where else she taught yoga, but she could not say due to a conflict of interest. That evening at the dinner table my mother said that she heard about an amazing woman named Tara Cindy Sherman who taught yoga at The Yoga Center of Minneapolis. Upon hearing this, I attended her yin-restorative yoga class that Sunday evening. Tara became my yoga teacher and mentor instantly. Eventually, I received my yoga teacher training at The Yoga Center of Minneapolis and took Tara's Radiant Shakti Flow Teacher Training course. Shakti Flow became a source of deeper awakening and remembrance in my life. Shakti Flow allowed the divine feminine energy to channel through me. It helped me to become empowered and assertive as a woman and stand firmly in my own feminine power. Today, I teach Radiant Shakti Flow to many women searching for such an awakening. My connection with Tara was no mistake.

During my time at The Emily Program, I communicated with my angels daily. While living in Oregon, I had learned that sugar and meat could harm my energetic body. This information heightened my fear of "bad" foods and weight gain. When the program meal plan required that I eat sugar and meat, my angels said my energy body was more affected by my thoughts, beliefs, and emotions than the foods I ate. They told me to bless my food and send it light before I ate it and have loving thoughts about the food and my body. They told me that food and body judgments were no longer serving me. I learned that unconditional love can transmute anything into light. I followed my heart, intuition, and angels rather than fear. I began to gain the physical strength I needed to recover. The cells of my body were transmuting from dark to light.

During the last day of treatment, each group member shares their personal story. I was terrified to share my story. The thought of talking to my group about what I had been through in the past year produced panic within me. I had not yet told a soul about my healing journey and my profound Reiki healing session. I wasn't ready to completely open up. I told as much of my story as I could.

June 23, 2011
Dear Group,

I am terrified to share my story. I have been through a lot this past year and I am not sure how much I want to reveal - how much is too fresh, too vulnerable to share. Part of my story I have shared with no one. I am not sure how to convey my path, so I have written some down and other parts I will simply speak from my heart. I want to say thank you for being here for me; this group has touched my life in many ways.

Through The Emily Program I learned about balanced nutrition, the benefits of having a meal plan, finding and maintaining a healthy weight, and self-care. I was able to restore my weight, enjoy new foods, and make new friends. I began to feel warmer and less anxious as time went on. I was feeling blessed to be alive, smell the fresh air, feel the grass on my feet, watch the birds soar through the sky, and swing to my heart's content.

After gaining forty pounds to return to a healthy weight and months of internal work, I could breathe, jump, swim, ride horseback, and play. But I gained a lot more than weight and physical strength. Eventually, I gained internal confidence and inner strength. I gained trust in my intuition and body. Ultimately, I came home to the inner dwelling of my soul which is much deeper than flesh and bones.

I started The Emily Program in May and by July I was volunteering with horses. I volunteered at the University of Minnesota Veterinary Medical Center. I spent time with horses that were sick and in need of love and attention. My deep love for horses began when I was eight years old. The strong, gentle, and sensitive creatures were my friends, teachers, and playmates. Horses have kept me grounded and calmed my emotions. I feel safe and loved around them. It had been several years since I had ridden a horse or spent quality time with one. Volunteering gave me the opportunity to reconnect with horses. Their magnificent spirits had always been healing for me and that summer was no exception. Little did I know that within months I would meet an angelic horse that would touch my heart and transform my world.

July 18, 2011
Dear Diary,

I am finding joy in each day, and I am finding happiness in the small things: being able to do warrior pose in the morning, seeing the birds while driving, and enjoying a cup of tea. I am smiling more and starting to feel connected to my body, Mother Earth, and humanity. I am beginning to listen to the sacred cues of my body's wisdom. Each day I feel safer in my own body and safer in the world. I hope to one day feel completely safe and at home in my body. Hope prevails, love is within, and smiles are healing. Each day I find something to smile about, appreciate, and enjoy in the life I am living.

Not only did I spend time with horses in July 2011, but I also had the strength to develop a daily yoga practice. Yoga entered my life when I was eighteen. My yoga path started as a pursuit of physical strength and flexibility and turned into a journey of opening my heart to the Light. That summer yoga not only grounded my spirit, but also helped my physical body renew and recharge.

I spent one week at my family cabin that summer on Lake Michigan in Door Country, Wisconsin. I was terrified to go swimming in Lake Michigan thinking my lungs might relapse. But I went anyway and loved it. My body was coming back to life, and I was beginning to enjoy movement again after two years of being sedentary. Each time I did a new activity, it felt like the first time I had ever done it. It truly felt like I was reborn.

That was a special week at my cabin. Not only was I able to reconnect with swimming but I also reconnected with my grandmother, Julie. One morning I woke early to the sounds of birds chirping. I got out of bed and sat on the couch where I could view Lake Michigan. It was a clear morning, the sun had just risen, and the lake was a beautiful deep blue. I opened my journal, grabbed my favorite pencil and began to write.

August 2, 2011
Dear Diary,

I am at my cabin in Door County, Wisconsin, and I feel my grandmother close. Every time I think of her, the frog in the chimney croaks and the birds chirp. I feel her as if she is sitting next to me. I feel her powerful yet gentle presence, and I feel her deep encouragement and everlasting support.

Grandma Julie died when I was in third grade. I remember it like it was yesterday. I vividly remember walking into the beautiful Unitarian Church and sitting in the second row for the funeral. Tears rolled down my cheeks and I felt like the whole church could see me. That night after her funeral I dreamt of a very tall staircase and at the top was my Grandma as an angel. It felt as though she was protecting me. I feel like she has been protecting and loving me on my long journey up the staircase to bliss within this lifetime. I can feel her this morning in my heart.

I spent one more day up at my parents' cabin after that special morning with Grandma Julie. Before I had left for the cabin that summer, I had a tattoo of a butterfly done on my left foot, on top of the spot that represents the left lung according to reflexology. The tattoo is a symbol of my beautiful wings (lungs), freedom from anorexia and fear, unconditional love, and inner bliss. I dedicated the tattoo to living in alignment with my heart, my soul, and my higher calling. Before having the tattoo done, I fed fish at the tattoo shop. As I poured the fish food into the clear water I made a dedication to live and act from my heart. Every time I look at my tattoo I smile.

That summer I also reconnected with an old cord. One sunny afternoon I was organizing my childhood bedroom, and I found an old cord in my dresser. The cord was from a summer trip to Camp Menogyn in high school. I had spent a month backpacking through Jasper, Canada. It was the trip of a lifetime. I went with five women and saw the Canadian Rockies along with other amazing sights. Spending a month in nature with women was empowering. Nature has always been my sacred home. Nature truly sees and understands me. After backpacking through beautiful Canadian mountains and sharing intimate moments together, we had a special ceremony around a candle. One woman would wrap a synthetic cord around another woman's wrist and would tell her what she had appreciated about her. Everyone in the circle experienced giving and receiving the cord. It was a special time in my life, and the cord meant a lot to me. It was a time in my life during which my self-esteem was very low, and hearing the encouragement and love from the other women was very powerful. When I found the cord in my dresser, I instantly wanted to wear it. I put it around my wrist and made an inward dedication. I dedicated the cord to living in alignment with my higher purpose, heart, and soul. Every time I look at this cord I am reminded of the dedication I made.

As I accept my challenges as stepping stones, see my setbacks as opportunities for greater expansion, and embrace my weaknesses, my heart-space begins to glow like the silver wings of an angel.

Loving the self begins with never ever criticizing ourselves for anything.
– Lousie Hay

Chapter 8

Silver Wings

August 7, 2011
Dear Diary,

When I am present with my angels I am completely in the moment, completely at peace, and my body is at ease. My breathing is relaxed, and I feel healthy. When I start to worry about my familial relationships or finances or having the responsibility of healing gifts or my outfit that day or who I am becoming, my breathing is not relaxed. It is time for me to release anxieties about making a mistake or not being good enough. I am learning to love myself unconditionally and let go of perfectionism. I am learning to give myself more space to be, truly be. My healing journey is a process, and I am learning to allow my path to unfold instead of trying to control it. I am learning to surrender and let go of control. I am learning to be gentle and kind with myself. Ultimately, I am learning to love myself unconditionally, the way my angels love me. My angels tell me to "see yourself and others through the lens of love. See past the illusions of the ego and into the heart. View others and yourself like we view you." The more I practice this, the more expansive my breath and wings become. I am transmuting fear into love, and my butterfly wings are expanding each day.

I first learned about angels through Louise Lavergne at Joyful Yoga in Jacksonville, Oregon. It was a sunny afternoon and I was walking from my apartment to the Joyful Yoga studio to meet with Louise. We had weekly sessions where she provided me with spiritual guidance. As I was walking I was reminded of Brooke's death. It had been a month since Brooke died and I felt her angelic presence often. That afternoon I was reminded of a dream I had of Brooke. There was a lot of crystal clear blue water in the dream. Brooke came to me in a very angelic form; she radiated white light. She said, "stand tall and be proud of who you are." She was helping me embrace my height and my path. At that moment I knew Brooke was like an angel.

As I entered the yoga studio that afternoon, Louise was waiting for me. We began by talking about how my chanting was going.

Louise gave me chants to say in the morning to help me awaken to my true nature. After discussing chanting, I told Louise that I felt Brooke's presence. Louise closed her eyes and took a deep breath. She said, "Brooke is with you right now. She is like one of your angels. She is very happy where she is. She finished what she came here to do." Louise was a medium, a person who communicates with the other side.

Then I asked Louise, "Do angels exist?" She said, "I believe in them." She told me to ask for their assistance and witness what happens. After that session with Louise, I began speaking to my angels and asking for their help. Miracles started happening. I asked the angels for a piece of fruit at work and a co-worker handed me an apple. I asked to connect more deeply with my heart, and during a meditation my heart started opening and I could feel intense sensations of Light around my heart center. I asked for clarity around my life purpose and a card came to me that said "healer and teacher." I asked about the Light and a friend gave me a book called *Living with Joy*, channeled by Sanya Roman. Her books became teachings on the Light for me. Through all of this, I was developing a deep connection with my angels.

After a year and a half of chanting, meditating, asking for the angels' assistance and receiving their guidance, I started to see angels. This began during the winter of 2009 after I became very ill. During meditation or time in nature, I would see my angels as huge beings of radiant light in my third eye. They were always with me and their teachings were about unconditional divine love. They were helping me open my heart to unconditional love for my illness and myself.

In January 2010 after a restless night hindered with difficulty breathing, I awoke to several angels next to me. A huge angel wrapped in golden light appeared above me. She brought me hope and faith. She reassured me that I would heal from my illness. She was a large omnipresent figure that filled my body with unconditional love. She was loving and gentle and brought me a sense of peace. Enveloped in her presence I felt the confidence that I could survive my challenging path. I knew my path on Earth would serve an important purpose, she offered the help to walk through it with grace and love. She gave me the courage to continue opening my heart and lungs.

After that mystical encounter with one of my angels, I began writing this book. I felt an enormous amount of energy surge through my entire body; I opened my laptop and my fingers moved quickly. I was sweating and my heart was expanding with sensations of tingling warmth. It felt as though my soul radiated from my heart onto these pages. Every time I wrote, I felt the presence of my soul, my heart, and my angels. Putting my story onto black and white has been a soul calling from the inner dwelling of my heart.

I not only sensed my angels deeply while I was writing, but also when I was in nature. The trees, the birds, the air, the water, they all washed away my fears and negative head spaces, and I was able to tap into my heart and the angelic realm more clearly. During the summer of 2011, I was walking around Lake of the Isles and I felt blessed to be alive. I felt very connected. I could feel the trees around me. I was able to receive clear guidance from the birds, and I felt a sense of peace when watching the glistening water sparkle. As I gazed into the magical water, I heard my angels speak. They said, "It is time to let go of your identity with your body and identify with the love and light that you are. Your true essence rests within not without. You are not your body, you are an omnipresent being filled with love and light." As they spoke to me, my heart palpitated with sensations of warmth, radiance, and expansion, and my whole body sweated profusely.

As time went on, the connection with my angels grew deeper, and I was hearing their messages more often. They were my allies, my support team. They loved me beyond words. I cherished the relationship I had developed with my angels, partly because it was internal and not external. In the earthly realm everyone saw me as a physical body. Everywhere I went people commented on my tall frame. Throughout my life I frequently heard, "Wow, you are so tall. How did you get so tall?" I was uncomfortable around humans because I feared their body-related comments. With the angels, that all disappeared. It was like with the animals; they didn't care what I looked like or what I was wearing. They loved me far beyond appearances. I felt my angels' true unconditional love daily. They never judged me.

In the fall of 2011, I was meditating in my Reiki room and sensed the presence of my angels within my heart. My angels spoke.

> Return your attention to love and compassion, and focus on the light within you and within others. Remember that only love is real, and if it is not love, it is an illusion. See others through the eyes of angels and send compassion, light, and love to them. Remember that if others are suffering, they need more love. Concentrate on your own beautiful light and know and believe you are wonderful just the way you are, and you do not have to prove yourself to others. Turn your attention towards animals, nature, or anything that brings you in harmony with your soul. Take care of your own life; stay in your own beautiful soul and shine that onto others. Send the darkness more light. To be of service means to stay in your heart-space and shine that onto others. That is true service.

This message helped me to let go of the need to prove myself to others and being concerned about their perception of me.

I ask the angels for daily assistance with work, body aches, and even little things like parking, and more. Their advice helps my days flow gracefully with more gentleness and ease. They are very gentle and their presence is soft, but powerful. Their nudges come when I am daydreaming or staring into the beautiful sky. I feel their presence more clearly when I am in nature, chanting, meditating, practicing Reiki, writing, or around animals. They are fairy-like.

They respect my decisions and never interfere with my free will, but when asked they truly help.

One morning after meditation I asked my angels, “What can I do for you? You have done so much for me.” They responded, “Publish your book.” I felt warmth and tingles throughout my entire being. This book has felt like a calling greater than me.

Connecting with my angels has been a remarkable journey. One that has brought more peace, joy, grace, and ease into my daily life. Through the angels’ support I have gained the courage to speak my truth and follow my dreams. Their support is unconditional and available to me at any moment. I have learned that we all have an abundance of support in the universe, we only need to ask for it. And when we say “thank you,” more support comes our way. The angels are only a whisper away. Their silver wings can be felt through the heart.

As I watch the colors, the varieties, and the textures that encompass the planet, I am reminded of the beauty of the whole. The strength of the trees reminds me of my courage, the flow of the river reminds me of my grace, and the sounds of the birds remind me of my own sensitivity.

CHAPTER 9

Butterflies, Dragonflies, and Bees

Beginning in the summer of 2009, butterflies appeared around me daily. They came in all shapes, colors, and sizes. I saw large and small, yellow, pink, blue, and red butterflies. Each encounter felt like a reunion with a long lost sister. They symbolized transformation, harmony, unconditional love, and awakening. They came to me as messengers from the divine saying, "You are transforming from the state of a caterpillar to a butterfly." The human butterfly state is one of awareness, unconditional love, and living from the heart.

Early that summer, I was walking in nature and found a butterfly with a broken wing. The butterfly's broken wing reminded me of my broken lung and how ill I was. I felt deep compassion for the butterfly and carried her home with me to nurse her back to health. I was almost home with the butterfly when a large gust of wind blew her out of my hands. She was gone in an instant. I released her to Spirit, remembering that all things come from Spirit and go back home to Spirit.

In addition to the connection I had developed with butterflies, I began connecting with other insects as well. In the summer of 2010, bees started coming to me. One day I was with Dena in Lithia Park. Dena was giving me Reiki to help with my healing. We were near a small pond and I was lying on the grass receiving the energy of Reiki. After my treatment we were talking about sharing Reiki with others in nature parks across the world. We were discussing the healing power of nature, and at that moment, a bee began circling me. Dena told me bees were symbols of the soul. That day I remembered clearly that my soul was here to help with the healing and awakening of humanity through nature and Reiki.

Later that summer, I was eating lunch with my brother on my parents' porch. My brother and I were discussing chanting and spirituality. I felt a bit reserved about telling my brother all of my spiritual experiences for fear of judgment. A bee began circling me, then landed on my lunch plate. It stayed there for a few minutes and then left. I smiled knowing it came to remind me of my soul purpose to speak my truth and share my heart regardless of others' judgments.

That summer also marked the appearance of the dragonfly. Dragonflies started landing on my chest, arm, and finger. They came so close to me that I could look them in the eye. Around the dragonflies I felt a sense of belonging. I felt at home and unconditionally accepted. They were also healing messengers from the divine. Their fragile, sensitive wings were beautiful and mystical. Around them I felt like I was in the physical presence of an angel.

I will never forget the day a dragonfly came to me as a living angel. It was a warm August day, and the sky was blue with vibrant white glowing clouds. I was painting and journaling on my parents' porch.

August 10, 2011
Dear Diary,

I am feeling like I have all this love inside and I want to share it. I want to share it with humanity. All beings deserve happiness, freedom, peace, joy, and unconditional love. Too many are suffering. I want to be the light I came here to be. I want to practice Reiki. I feel a very deep call within to pursue Reiki. There is still fear, still doubt shadowing me, shadowing my truth. I need courage now to break through and to live out my dream, to do what I came here to do. I feel my soul, and I can feel my call. Reiki means so much to me.

I put down my pencil for a moment, and I had the urge to call Linda. I picked up the phone and dialed her number. Within seconds she answered; it felt so good to hear her voice. I always felt safe with Linda. I could speak to her straight from my heart. She was truly a miracle in my life. That afternoon on the phone with Linda I had an opening. I began speaking to her about my Reiki healing, my hands heating up when performing Reiki, and the inner calling within my heart to pursue Reiki. At one point I was sobbing. I told her that my heart had been calling me to do Reiki for a long time and I had resisted, I was afraid. Tears rolled down my cheeks as I told her my heart ached to perform Reiki and I knew it was part of my deeper purpose. But I was terrified. What if no one comes, what if no one feels the energy I feel...what if, what if, what if? I was scared of others judging Reiki as unreal or weird. I was terrified, but I knew that if I died tomorrow, I wanted to perform Reiki today. Reiki was that important to me, and I wanted to answer the call of my heart.

Linda reassured me; she told me I was extremely gifted and I would be able to help many, many people after going through what I went through. She told me that it is always scary to start something new. She said, "Start, even though you have fears and doubts. Start and do not worry if others can't feel the energy, know that you can feel it." As I was processing these encouraging words from Linda, a dragonfly landed on the flower next to me. Studying the dragonfly's golden wings, I felt a powerful sensation within my heart-space, and it was at this moment that I decided to follow my heart's calling to be a Reiki healer.

Linda told me that dragonflies were a symbol of transcendence. I was transcending from fear to love. For several days after my phone conversation with Linda, I wrote in my journal.

August 11, 2011
Dear Diary,

Disease is misalignment with your spirit. Our actions are either aligned with our heart and spirit or aligned with illusion and/or external desires. When I was consumed with running and my physical body, I wasn't in alignment with my spirit and heart. As I heal, nurture my mind, body, and spirit, and practice the art of unconditional love for others and myself, I begin to align with my soul and regain my health. As I pursue my heart's calling to practice Reiki, I feel fulfilled and my physical body begins to radiate health.

The more I love myself and give myself what I need, the more I am able to do true service work. I am here to heal myself and help others heal. Reiki has been a huge influence on my healing path, one of the most profound influences in my life, and in my heart I feel extremely connected to Reiki. The more I listen to my intuition and my heart, the more I feel free and truly content. During Reiki sessions I become very hot and my hands radiate with energy. I often start sweating and tingling, and I can feel my heart open and expand. I feel relaxed yet energized and the sessions give me more energy. I am excited to continue to pursue my Reiki trainings, studies, and practice. I love feeling so connected to something greater than me. This healing journey has become more than I ever expected it to be. I am growing, expanding, and becoming more in tune than ever before.

August 12, 2011
Dear Diary,

It's 4:01 a.m. The streets are dark and silence abounds. My two kitties are purring and I am awake. My hands type away on my computer. I am the only one awake in the home; my night light is lit and my body lies on my comfortable bed which was brought all the way from Oregon. My feet hang off a little as I am six feet tall. My blonde hair falls past my shoulders. The purring of my kitties calms and reassures me. They help me stay in the present moment. As my fingers feel the softness and gentleness of my kitties, my gaze softens and my hearts feels more at peace. This moment seems to last forever, each minute as long as some hours.

In September 2011 I began telling people closest to me that I practice Reiki. I transformed my childhood bedroom into a Reiki studio. I put my most healing paintings on the wall, brought in my massage table, and bought roses, candles, and essential oils. I spent a week meditating, walking in nature, asking the universe for assistance, and clearing my Reiki studio. Within days after it was clear, I had clients on my massage table; my healing energy flowed stronger than ever before. At times my body and hands became extremely hot and I sweated and felt tingling in my body throughout the whole session.

Over the years I have learned I channel Reiki energy and an abundance of pure love and light. In the summer of 2014 I spoke with Dr. Katherine who said, "You are not only a channel of Reiki energy, but a pure channel of an abundance of source energy. Your physical body is vibrating at a very high level and you are bringing pure love and light to humanity." The same week, Catie Sanburg, an energy healer who I saw regularly for support, said, "Reiki was your opening to your calling of energy healing. You channel pure source energy. You are vibrating at a high rate and it is very important for you to have boundaries with everyone in your life to stay in your own energy field." I follow my higher calling each day and have dedicated my healing gifts to the greater good of humanity.

Most of my life I have felt unique and sensitive. I felt and sensed the non-physical realms. I started to see my gifts as a miracle. I started feeling blessed, abundant, and fully supported by the universe and thankful for my sacred gifts. My connection with angels, Reiki, butterflies, insects, animals, nature, and Spirit is extremely strong, partly because of my sensitivity. I have learned that my sensitivity is not a weakness but a strength.

As I greet my fuzzy friends with open arms and feel the bricks of lead fall away, I begin to span my wings. As I listen to the purr of the kitties and watch the wonder of the horses, I begin the process of learning to fly.

CHAPTER 10

Bliss

In the fall of 2011, I spent my time practicing Reiki, receiving massages, horseback riding, painting, writing, listening to music, walking, and making new friends. My passion for horses fully reemerged. As a child I went to the barn almost every day to horseback ride, and I rode horses throughout high school as well. Horses were my companions. I understood them and they understood me. I loved touching their soft velvet noses, brushing their beautiful manes, and galloping through the fields on their back. I felt accepted and embraced around horses. Some of my most memorable times from childhood are of horseback riding through pristine fields. As I grew older and went away to college to pursue nursing and cross-country running, I did not have time for riding. I always missed it and dreamt of doing it again one day. That time had finally come during the fall of 2011. I told my physician assistant at The Emily Program of my desire to ride, and she said I was able to do it physically. I was nervous to overexert my lungs, but I followed my deep inner desire to be on a horse again.

I researched different barns on the internet and found an affordable one. When I first entered the barn and saw all of the wonderful healthy horses, my heart pounded with bliss. I instantly fell in love with the barn and the horses.

At first trotting around the ring was exhausting for me. Mounting and riding the horse took strength and muscles I had not used in years. I took three-hour naps on the days I went riding. During the first month at the barn, I rode a reliable, steady, white horse. He was perfect for me to begin with. I had not ridden in nine years, and I was coming back after being terribly ill. He was gentle and allowed me to gain my strength slowly. Being around the horses, smelling them, grooming them, and riding them brought me the same sense of love, joy, and peace that I had experienced with my angels. That fall the barn became my sacred haven. When I was around the horses, my fears seemed to disappear, and I became at peace and in the moment. Worries about my lungs relapsing diminished when I was on the horse. Horseback riding was my gateway back to physical strength.

Six weeks had passed since I first stepped foot at my new barn. I was riding two to three times a week, and I was gaining strength. My naps after riding went down from three hours to one hour, then from thirty minutes to not needing a nap at all. I was feeling strong and confident, and I was ready for a new horse to ride. I was ready to have a deep, heartfelt, spiritual connection with a horse. I started watching all the horses in the field. I asked my riding friends about the different horses that were at the barn. I asked, who is a thoroughbred? Who has a fiery nature? Who is sweet? A friend told me about Kestrel, Rose Mare, and Jackpot. Kestrel approached me one day while I was in the field. Instantly, I felt a connection. He was a chestnut beauty with white socks and a white stripe on his forehead. Every time I went into the field I found him and spent time getting to know him. Then one night I had a dream about him. In this dream we had bonded. After that I decided I wanted to ride him. I told some of the other riders what I wanted to do. One friend at the barn said she did not think the riding teacher would allow me to ride Kestrel because I just started to ride again after taking so many years off and Kestrel was a more challenging horse. When Kestrel first arrived at the barn, he was very thin and highly skittish. The riding instructor fell off of him and broke his collarbone. My friend did not think I was ready to ride Kestrel. Regardless of what my friend thought, I knew I had a deep connection to Kestrel. I really wanted to ride him, so one beautiful morning when I was on a trail ride behind my instructor, I looked into the sky and my angels gave me guidance to ask about riding Kestrel. The instructor agreed to let me try, and I was thrilled. I eagerly waited for the next lesson. The lesson day came, and I was overjoyed to see him. As I prepared to ride him, I felt a resonance with him, a genuine connection. I was elated being around him. There was a rhythm when I rode him. In the months to come he became a treasured, heartfelt friend. We were kindred spirits.

Kestrel brought me deep peace and healing. He showed me unconditional love. Around him I felt safe. He felt like one of my angels. When I rode him I was completely in the moment, and my mind was still. I did not worry about my lungs relapsing around Kestrel. Riding him allowed me to gain my endurance back. Riding Kestrel also brought me serenity. I was anxiety prone, but around Kestrel I felt calm and at ease. The rhythm while galloping through the fields, the beauty of the landscape, and the heart connection to him and the nature around us was very relaxing and therapeutic for me. My body began to remember ease and radiant health.

I started riding Kestrel three times a week and could not wait to do more with him. Through riding Kestrel I completely regained my health and physical strength. I felt a very deep spiritual connection to him. He had a spark; he was half Arabian and half saddle bred, and I loved this. I did not have to say anything and yet he understood me. I felt supported by him. His mane had highlights, his chestnut coat was gorgeous, and his white socks reminded me of my kittens. I was falling in love and following my bliss.

My connection with Kestrel grew deeper and more profound over the years. I started to lease him in January 2012 and rode him as much as I could. On him I felt strong, around him I felt safe, and no matter where I was, I always felt unconditionally loved by him. We truly were kindred spirits, and we unconditionally supported each other. When I was having a bad day, he would come up to me from the field and put his nose on my heart. He soothed my pain. I taught him to run next to me on the ground. We would play together. On one particular ride through the pasture with Kestrel, I saw a bald eagle sitting on a log several feet from us. It was magical. The bald eagle came to us to give me the courage to speak from my heart. Every day with Kestrel was a magical day. We cared deeply for each other. He came to me in my dreams telling me to follow my heart-space. He was helping me awaken to my soul and higher calling. He stood by me as I spoke from my heart and expanded my wings.

In January 2014 Kestrel got a respiratory infection and it exacerbated his heaves (horse asthma). This affected me deeply as I knew what it was like to have breathing difficulties. I was very concerned for him and only walked him in the ring. I rode him bareback with a halter. I could tell he was more comfortable without the bit. I knew he preferred to be bitless. I did not want to make him any more uncomfortable than he already was. Natural horsemanship had been in my heart for many years, and through Kestrel's lung infection, it was coming to fruition. I started to read and watch videos about people who rode with no bit or saddle. This intrigued and inspired me because I knew Kestrel preferred no bit. I wanted to respect and honor him. He had done so much for me, and I wanted to do anything I could for him. He was calmer and happier without the bit. Our connection and trust grew deeper through letting go of the bit. While galloping through the pasture with no bit we felt at ease, one with each other, confident, and calm. I fully understood his nature and honored him. We had a deep heart bond that was beyond the external. As I was learning to respect my body, I was also learning to honor his body and the nature all around me. Through letting go of the bit, I was learning to let go of the other things in my life that were symbols of the bit. I let go of shoes that hurt my feet and did not honor my body. I let go of any constricting clothing or disrespectful body comments. I was also letting go of others around me who did not truly honor or value me. Through letting go of the bit, I was respecting Kestrel's sacred vehicle as well as mine.

After letting go of the bit, I knew I had to confront the owner of the barn and Kestrel. I was terrified to tell him I wanted to ride Kestrel exclusively with no bit and no saddle. The little girl within me was scared of rejection and judgment. My inner child was scared, but I knew I had to find the courage to tell him of my new adventures with Kestrel.

On a sunny spring day in 2014 I went to the barn to ride Kestrel. The sun was brilliant in the sky, the birds were chirping, and Kestrel's owner was in the barn aisles assisting the farrier. He was in a pleasant mood and not busy with a riding lesson. I felt a strong urge to talk to him about riding Kestrel with no bit. The urge was so intense that I could not resist it.

I approached him and said, "I have been riding Kestrel with no bit and no saddle."

He said, "We've noticed that."

I said, "I noticed Kestrel prefers to be ridden this way."

He said, "I'm sure he prefers no bit, but the saddle distributes the weight over their back so it's more comfortable for them. Riding with a saddle is much better for their back muscles. If you can tighten the girth very gently and use treats, he might be okay with that."

Then, something came over me I did not expect. I told him how profoundly healing Kestrel had been for me and I started crying. "I had a traumatic childhood and Kestrel has been extremely healing for me. I want him to be comfortable while I ride him because I love him and care a lot about him." I said, "I did not expect this to come out."

He said, "This happens around horses, and that is too bad about your childhood."

I said, "I would like to always ride with no bit."

He said, "If Kestrel cooperates for you this way, that's fine, but you have already had a jumping accident and I think using the saddle would be safer. No bit is fine."

"I will give it a try," I said.

That afternoon I practiced jumping Kestrel with a saddle, but no bit. Kestrel was calm as I put the saddle and girth on, and he loved jumping. He was comfortable with the saddle and no bit. I found a way to jump and trail ride that was comfortable for both of us. We were in bliss.

Through Kestrel I have learned that opening up and showing your true colors can reveal a world of possibilities and bring you closer to people you never thought possible. I have also learned that each set of horse and rider are a unique pair. Each horse and rider has their own unique journey.

Kestrel is an honest friend. He tells me what makes him uncomfortable, he loves me unconditionally, and he supports me through thick and thin. Every day I am grateful to have found Kestrel. He has been a strong source of healing, friendship, and unconditional love in my life. He has taught me that true love exists, love beyond conditions.

As I align myself more clearly than ever before with my heart-space, and live with humility, grace, and compassion, I am reminded of my own eternal freedom, my true heart-space, and I begin to believe that each living creature is only a heartbeat away from flying FREE.

CHAPTER 11

A Broken Bone, an Alive Wound, and a Hopeful Spirit

It was Thursday, July 12, 2012, and I was sitting in traffic. I was driving to my favorite place, the barn. I usually did not horseback ride in the Thursday afternoon lesson, but another rider called and said she would not be riding. I took advantage of the open spot and drove there after work. Kestrel had a sore on his left side, so I knew I would not be riding him. The traffic was so terrible that I wasn't sure I would make it to the barn on time for the jumping lesson. Several times I thought about turning around and heading for home. But something inside of me wanted to get to the barn that evening, I was determined. I arrived about fifteen minutes before the start of the lesson.

After arriving I found out that Cody and Rose Mare were the horses available to ride. I choose Rose Mare, a younger, challenging horse. I had never ridden her, but her frisky spirit and wild nature excited me and gave me a challenge that was inspiring. I could not find Rose Mare in the field, but Kestrel came up to me. It was so nice to see him, and I wanted to ride him, but I told him I would ride him bareback after the lesson, so his sore would heal. When I found Rose Mare, Kestrel followed us to the front of the pasture. I had a hard time leaving him. The bond I created with Kestrel has been the strongest one I have ever formed with a horse. I feel incredibly safe and unconditionally loved with him. Even when I am not in his presence I can sense his sweetness and playfulness. He brings so much joy to my life, and I am so grateful for the connection I have created with him.

While preparing to ride Rose Mare, I did not feel a connection to her. The entire time I was thinking I would rather be riding Kestrel. Although, once I got on Rose Mare I began to have fun. She had very smooth gates and a fiery edge that I enjoyed, temporarily. I was just getting comfortable on her when we started the jumping portion of the lesson. We started with a bounce, which is three jumps in a row. The first set was fun and I wanted more. The second set was even better. Then, our instructor asked us to jump a difficult combination – two jumps in a row and then the third jump quickly off to the side. I watched my friends jump the combination and everyone was having trouble. At that point I really wanted to be on Kestrel. I did not trust that Rose Mare and I would make it through that type of combination; it was too challenging for us, as it was my first time riding her. I did not feel comfortable riding her at that level of difficulty, but I did not voice my concern to my instructors. I have always been perceived as a strong, capable, competent woman, and I did not want to let down my instructors or the group by saying that the jump was too difficult. So we proceeded ahead. I envisioned us making it over, but the vision was blurry. We circled once before the combination. We made it over the first two jumps safely. Then, I saw a tall standard, hit the ground, and thought, "This can't be true. No! This can't be happening, not now. This must be a dream. Please, no, this is a dream! I do not want this!" I thought of my plan to go to the barn and ride Kestrel every day in July. I was on the ground and could not move. The emotional pain set in first, and later the excruciating physical pain came.

I lay on the ground, tears streaming down my face, more so from the emotional upset than the physical discomfort. After several minutes I was able to stand. One of my instructors walked me inside and gave me some ice. I felt the pain in my left arm and thought it was broken. I cried and told her how devastated I was, and she consoled me. I told her about my pneumonia and my healing connection with Kestrel. I did not want to be injured, not again. She suggested we go to urgent care. As I stood up to get in the car, we noticed that there was a lot of bleeding coming from my left thigh. My leg hurt but I had no idea how severe the injury was.

As I was wheeled into a room at the urgent care center, I saw a poster that said "Spirit is your rock." At that moment I knew this injury was aligning me even closer to Spirit. The doctor at urgent care said my left thigh wound was too deep to sew up, and I needed to go to the emergency room. As my riding instructor drove me to the nearest hospital, I felt dizzy from the loss of blood, and I was a bit nervous. I drank as much water as I could. My mother and brother met us at the emergency room, and I said goodbye to my instructor. It took some time to get in to see a doctor, and we were getting concerned. I was bleeding heavily which caused a puddle of blood underneath my wheelchair. The nurses did not realize the severity of the injury and once they did, they called a trauma alert. Within minutes, I was seen by a doctor and started on IV fluids. They took an x-ray and gave me a strong pain reliever for the intense pain that began after the endorphin rush ended.

My left arm had a broken radial head, my left upper thigh had a wound that was three and a half inches deep by five inches wide, and I was being prepared for surgery. I had never had surgery before and had always been terrified of the thought of it. However, in the midst of a trauma and serious bleeding, the prospect of surgery did not faze me. At 1 a.m. on July 13, 2012 I met my surgeon. He was tall, dark, and handsome. His energy was gentle, yet strong, and he radiated confidence. I asked him, "Are you awake enough to do surgery on my thigh?" He said, "I just drank a 16 ounce cup of coffee. I am completely awake." I put my faith in him. As I was wheeled down to the surgery room, I put one hand on my heart and one hand on my belly. I asked for assistance from the higher realms. Before I entered the surgery room my mom whispered in my ear, "Malachim," which is Hebrew for "the angels are protecting you." I felt a sense of peace wash over me as they rolled me into the operating room.

Two hours later I woke in the recovery room. I had oxygen in my nose and I was anxious. I was wondering what happened in surgery and wanted to speak with my mom. They wheeled me up to the third floor of the hospital where I met my mom. I asked her, "What did the surgeon tell you, and when can I ride Kestrel again?" She said it would take one year for full recovery. My heart sank and I started sobbing. One year. I thought, "No way, this must be a dream, how can I handle taking one whole year off of horseback riding?" I was devastated.

The next morning I decided to think I was going to heal in three to six months, despite what the surgeon said, because that made me happy. That morning I also found out that the hospital offered other treatment options including healing touch, acupuncture, guided imagery, and essential oils. This lifted my spirits. That day I received acupuncture and healing touch, which relieved the pain and enhanced my energy. The healing touch took me to a place of deep peace and I felt no pain for two hours. I did energy healing on myself every day, which greatly assisted in the healing and growing of the wound tissue. I also listened to guided imagery tapes, which became a staple in my life. I was feeling very nauseated from the anesthesia and pain medication, so my nurse gave me ginger essential oil which was helpful.

My hospital stay lasted five days. Before this event I had fear around being a patient in the hospital; by the end I had no fear. Besides having a huge wound, fainting twice from loss of blood, and feeling very nauseated from pain medication, my hospital stay was positive. The nurses and doctors were amazing. My evening nurse cheered me up every time I saw her. I felt safe and supported by her. I fainted in my mother's arms one evening and she came to my rescue. My acupuncturist also cheered me up each day. I felt a connection to him, and his presence was very healing. I trusted my surgeon and each doctor I met, which was comforting. Being a nurse myself, I am particular about medical professionals and was extremely pleased with the care I received.

The wound nurse was also wonderful. He decided my wound was a candidate for a wound vac, which he applied. Although I was hooked to IVs and a drainage system, I was healing and even smiling at times. My brother made me laugh, and my mother pushed me in a wheelchair outside by the healing gardens where I saw butterflies and dragonflies. During my hospital stay I felt protected and guided by many angels. Many people told me how lucky I was that the wound did not damage muscles, tendons, or my femur. The staff repeatedly complimented me on my positive attitude. Despite the devastation of the accident and losing horseback riding, I was finding joy within each day. My connection with my angels brought me a deep sense of unconditional love.

After my hospital stay I returned to my parents' home. When I arrived, it took all my energy to make it down the stairs. My left side was very weak from the wound and broken arm. My body was still recovering from the loss of blood, causing frequent dizziness. I decided to stay in my Reiki room where I had cultivated an abundance of healing energy. Once I got settled, I focused on staying rested. I spent time listening to audio books by Sanya Roman on becoming your true soul identity. I meditated often and went within. I would feel my heart-space and the presence of my angels. I worked with my angel cards, and the message I received was that my injury was a blessing in disguise. I did a lot of energy healing on myself, and every day I listened to guided imagery. It was a rejuvenating time for me. I received a Reiki session from a Reiki Master, and she said my body was recalibrating to a higher frequency through this injury. She said my body was realigning and my physical structure was going to be stronger because of the injury. She also said I was developing new DNA in my bone marrow that was of a higher vibration. She said this injury was a blessing and part of my spiritual path. I felt at peace knowing this information.

One week after I left the hospital I saw my surgeon. He took an x-ray of my broken arm and viewed my wound. He said I was healing quickly. I asked, "How long do you think it will be before I can ride Kestrel?" He said three months was a great goal as my wound was healing extraordinarily fast. My eyes lit up. He said I could go visit Kestrel any time and start walking. After that appointment I immediately went to the barn to see Kestrel. I was glowing with happiness. I had a great time seeing my friends at the barn. I spent an hour connecting with Kestrel, rubbing his velvet nose, giving him carrots, and loving him. My friends at the barn were amazed at how well I looked. I knew it was because of the Reiki. After that day I was able to go for very slow, gentle nature walks and visit Kestrel a couple times a week. Slowly, steadily I became stronger in every way.

Shortly after the riding accident, I had an epiphany; I thought, if I am going to continue living on Earth, I want to enjoy life to its fullest, no matter what. I realized that I did not want to waste my precious time feeling self-pity, judging myself, or feeling victimized. Instead, I wanted to put my energy and time into the things that bring me joy and a positive mindset. The small things in the hospital made my days enjoyable, such as watching a deer outside my window or joking and laughing about the hospital panties being sexy. My accident was truly a blessing. I learned to trust my body's innate wisdom and healing powers, and I learned the beauty, strength, and magic of my body. I learned that I could find joy in the simple pleasure of resting.

My riding accident taught me to see beyond the illusion of good and bad or right and wrong. Many said my accident was "bad," yet I grew and expanded from the experience, which was positive. At a surface level, the accident appeared misfortunate, yet at a deep spiritual level I was elevating my vibration and transforming. The physical world is often a catalyst for spiritual evolution and growth. Behind the physical veil we cannot fully see the light. Once the veil is shed we can see the richer layers of spiritual expansion at play. It is through the window of the heart that we can see clearly. The mind is hidden behind a veil of good/bad and right/wrong, but the heart feels the higher purpose. Through my accident I was able to expand my appreciation and love for my body, and the hours of stillness brought me to a new heightened spiritual state. My profound connection with my angels deepened.

My physical wounds and the wounds within my inner child were mending. My inner child went through trauma like my thigh did, and she had been bleeding for a very long time. She was mending and healing. Not only was I nourishing my wound back to radiant health, but I was nourishing my inner child as well. I was giving her the love and nourishment she deserves.

My wound completely healed within three months, and I was riding Kestrel again. Slowly I regained my physical strength, and I became stronger than before my accident. I continued loving myself the best I could, writing loving affirmations daily, keeping a gratitude and self-love journal, and remembering that bliss and health were my birthright. As time went by I became stronger and stronger. I was aligning more and more with my soul essence. When I chanted in the morning I would feel tingles throughout my body and feel my soul entering into me through my crown chakra. My healing practice was growing; I became a yoga teacher and a Reiki hospice nurse, starting a Reiki program for the hospice home care agency I worked for. I learned the importance of energetic boundaries. Each day I continued to grow spiritually, emotionally, mentally, and physically.

As I remember the joy of running, the beauty of muscles, and the strength within my heartbeat, I eagerly await the moment of dirt in my face, trails beneath my running shoes, and wind across my cheeks.

CHAPTER 12

The Beauty of Muscles

My heart-space has guided me back to running. In the spring of 2013 on a warm sunny day I was sitting in my therapist's office at The Emily Program. I told my therapist months before that I wanted to run again and she advised me not to. She knew how addictive running was for me in the past and how much it played into my anorexia. She told me the story about an experiment where they gave mice a wheel to run on, and the mice overran themselves to death. The mice had become addicted to running and prioritized running over eating. At that time I listened to the advice of my therapist and I did not begin running again. A feeling of deep longing to run would surface in my heart occasionally but I would suppress it. After meeting Gabriel, one of my angels, I had the courage to listen to my soul desire to run. On that warm sunny day I told my therapist I wanted to run. I told her my desire to run was not coming from my ego but from my heart, and I could feel it within the sensations of my heart-space. I told her I would still be at peace and happy if I never ran again, but reclaiming running in a new way would be empowering for me physically and for my soul. I wanted to experience running in a balanced way on Earth. My therapist said I should listen to my heart and not to her, which is exactly what I did. I began running again that spring. I started with easy jogs around Lake of the Isles. Gabriel, my angel, would come with me, and she wore beautiful pink running shoes.

The first time I ran around the whole lake I felt empowered. I felt free, completely recovered from my lung illness and very strong. Running slowly integrated back into my life, but in a very new form. I went for walks and jogs. I would go at a slow, comfortable pace and notice the birds along the way. I would stop anytime I was uncomfortable and I would only run when my body wanted to. I knew I was healed from my addiction to running when I could enjoy the blissful movement of running without becoming attached or dependent on it. I never overran, and I allowed my body to guide the way, not my mind. I ran for pure and simple love and joy, nothing else. I ran with peace and gentleness. It was wonderful.

I no longer identify myself as a runner, but as a spiritual, angelic being of love and light. When I was addicted to running, I missed out on the connection I now have with my inner world and the spiritual world. Now I feel the presence of my soul, whether I am sitting on a rock by the river, watching birds soar through the sky, running through green fields, grooming Kestrel, galloping with Kestrel through pastures, holding the space of a dying hospice patient, teaching yoga, practicing Reiki, driving in traffic, bundled inside during a Minnesota winter storm, or watching the magic of the clouds. Wherever I am, I am. When I finally let go of my external "runner" identity, judgments, and my ego, I was able to fully be my gentle, creative, playful, extremely heartfelt, loving soul. My identity has shifted from the external world to the spiritual world, from runner to angelic presence, from tall to beautiful large wingspan, from woman to divine feminine essence.

Journal entries from my trip to Patagonia, Chile

January 28, 2004
Dear Diary,

Sounds of laughter and music fill the air. I am in my fourth day of mountaineering. My tent is my home for now. Being here is part of my journey; each day I am changing. Every morning I wake up with one challenge ahead of me and each night I fall asleep with one challenge past me. The people here range from young to old, east to west, passive to aggressive. Each individual here has something to offer me, whether it is a life-long lesson or a moment of laughter. As I continue to write, the mountain views surround me and I am excited to embrace whatever the future may hold.

February 22, 2004
Dear Diary,

The sun is beating down on my already burnt nose, yet the cool air of the glacier keeps my body core colder than normal. Today was a day of ropes, lines, commands, and steps. At times I felt I was in a winter wonderland. Each snowflake reminded me that life is filled with mystery and magic. The rhythm of the terrain, my rope team, and my body seemed to work as one. Today I realized that each step along the way really does make a difference, whether it is a step in snow, water, or dirt or a step through life.

March 11, 2004
Dear Diary,

Each stroke I take, I become more in tune with this magical boat carrying my body through the rough waters. This kayak has become an extension of my body. It moves with me, speaks to me, feels me. The rain continues to drip off my paddle onto my arms, and the cold wind continues to hit my cheeks. The weather patterns are consistent, cold and rainy, and the bumpy waves hit hard. Each day is filled with rubber boots, tarps, and wet socks. The layers of poly pro and fleece keep my body core warm. Each day I am reminded that I am an internal heater. The daily routine of packing, paddling and cooking is cleansing for my system.

I have come to realize that my dedication to running and developing my athletic abilities among the outdoors has transformed into the dedication I now have to following my heart and higher calling. Energy does not disintegrate, it simply transforms. To cultivate internal strength, patience, spiritual connection, awareness, compassion, and unconditional love, dedication, persistence, and determination are vital. These traits are equally important when training to be a competitive athlete. When we dedicate ourselves to what matters most, our world will transform.

Cultivation of Unconditional Love

I have been on a journey of cultivating unconditional love for myself. Just as the soil must be dug, churned, and tilled in a garden, I have dug deep into my soul, weeded my thoughts, tilled my energy, and planted seeds of radiant health. The garden of my heart becomes more beautiful every day. The more I write in my self-love journal, practice loving daily affirmations, remind myself that I am lovable just the way I am, and open to the love of my angels, the more love flows through me. I have learned that I am either in alignment with my heart or with a fear or judgment. As I choose to align myself with my heart daily, the roses of my life blossom. One of my favorite insights is that we all deserve unconditional love just the way we are. If we are on the planet, we deserve pure, radiant love. The plants and animals do not have to prove themselves or do anything to receive love. We can receive love just the way we are. I spent years thinking that I had to do something or find a trait about myself that was worthy of receiving love. Today, I know I deserve love because I am here, I am a child of the universe. Each day I give myself more and more love. I greet my body each morning with love in the mirror. My body judgments of the past continue to wash away, and I consistently tell my body how much I love it. I feed it nourishing foods and listen to its precious messages. When my body signals hunger, I eat the most nourishing, lovable ingredients possible. When my body signals full, I stop. Through the years I have learned which foods support my body and help my body feel happy, calm, and filled with positive energy. As my body changes every day, I change with it and listen to which foods and playful movements it truly needs for support and energy. Every day I consciously choose body love and body nourishment. I bless my food and see it as living love entering my body. I listen to my body's signals for rest and sleep when needed. I run when my body has the energy to run and stop when my body needs to walk. I see each moment as an opportunity to love myself and my body more. I care for my body with loving essential oils, pure lotions, herbal teas, Epsom bath salts, organic castor oil packs, massages, facials, and organic skin care. I dress my body with playful colors and loving, soft fabrics. My body was judged extremely harshly in childhood and into early adulthood by myself and others. Now I want to give my body the love it deserves in all forms. We are all worthy of unconditional love from ourselves and the world just the way we are today. We all have the capacity within us to cultivate unconditional love for ourselves and our bodies. I have dedicated my life to unconditional love.

September 23, 2013
Dear Diary,

The enormous, beautiful pink butterfly who has come to me many times before in meditation was flying above me. Her silver, iridescent wings were eagle-like and her left wing was fully repaired. Her wings soared and her strong, thick feet were carrying a book called "The Beauty of Wings." She wanted me to deliver this book to the world.

January 31, 2015
Dear Diary,

I have awakened to the beautiful pink butterfly within me which had been there all along. She is my soul. I have accessed the unconditional love within my heart and soul beyond height, weight, eye color, skin color, and external measures. From an excruciatingly painful childhood to anorexia to suffocation to near death, I have found the beauty of my wings and true freedom. I have been able to reclaim running in a healthy way. My lungs are healed, my wings are expanded, I am free of anorexia and inhalers, and each day I am grateful for my breath and ability to run freely. I grow and learn each day. I continue to evolve. Each day my body becomes more healthy and radiant. My angels are my sisters. I will allow my heart-space to shine freely.

April 14, 2015
Dear Diary,

I have come home to my natural state of bliss. My connection with Mother Earth has become incredibly strong. She brings me unlimited joy and nourishment, and I feel one with Her. I can sense Her presence and understand Her precious messages. My magical connection with Her and Kestrel becomes stronger every day.

As I allow the emphasis on the physical (height, weight, running times, skin color, body shape, etc.) to fall away, I turn inward to a much more beautiful place; one of unconditional love, complete acceptance, limitless joy, a place beyond right and wrong. This place rests within my heart, and as I live from here I feel true connection to my soul and the Light. From this place I can truly connect. I have been propelled to see beyond the surface and travel deep into the radiant layers of my heart.

As a child I was drowning in the waters of judgment, ridicule, and painful exclusion. My natural state – one of sensitivity, kindness, creativity, heart centeredness, and originality – was mocked growing up. No matter where I went I was seen as too tall, too sensitive, and too original. As I grew spiritually and turned inward to my heart filled with unconditional love for my inner child and myself, I grew radiant wings which propelled me out of murky waters into a butterfly state of freedom, harmony, joy, and unconditional love.

I was an indigo child; a child with a heightened intuition, sensitivity to nature and the spirit realms, extremely creative and artistic, and very playful. My parents, brother, teachers, coaches, and peers tried to suppress me into the boundaries of societal norms. As a result, I felt there must be something fundamentally "wrong" with me. Through my deep spiritual journey I came to know and understand unconditional love, and I learned my true nature is one of pure love and light and that there is nothing "wrong" with me. I learned judgments and the material world are illusions and clarity rests within the heart. Within all of us there is a place of love and light, a place of true beauty and freedom. We all deserve unconditional love.

The energy of the heart is available for us all to access. We can shift our sight from the material to the heart. From the heart we can clearly see.

After reading *Loving Yourself to Great Health* by Louise Hay, Ahlea Khadro, and Heather Dane, I began to love my body even more. Louise Hay taught me to run to the mirror every morning and greet myself with exclamations of "I love you" and "what can I do to make you happy today." I posted a letter to my body on my mirror:

Dear Body,

I love you dearly, I love every inch of you. I have a happy, healthy body filled with loving energy. It is my joy to love you to radiant health. The more I love you, the healthier I feel. My body is such a good friend, we have a great life together. I love and appreciate my beautiful body just the way it is. I rejoice that I have chosen this particular body because it is perfect for me. I love and approve of myself. I am safe to be me. I am safe in this body. I am wonderful just the way I am. I choose joy and self-acceptance.

This letter is from the book *Loving Yourself to Great Health.* However, I edited it slightly to meet my specific needs. When we love our body, our body responds with energy, joy, and health. Just as an animal responds well to love and affection, our body does too. I have learned that our soul choses our particular body for our soul purpose. There is no need to resist our chosen body, we can embrace it and our soul calling.

Forgiveness will set you free. Through the process of forgiving my family, I have learned that forgiveness is setting me free too. I have forgiven my family, which means I had to come to understand where their painful actions come from and wish them healing and awakening. My heart hopes for deep healing and awakening within each human being, including my family members. My heart sends light and love to all, even those that have hurt me deeply, and in return I am free to fly and spread my wings.

It is time for unconditional love. I invite you to open your heart to unconditional love and find the beauty of your own wings.

Transformation from fear to unconditional love is the path of awakening. When we see with the heart, spread our wings, and learn to fly, we become beings of radiant light.

May one day all human beings cultivate their wings and take flight.

A Final Note from the Author

The journey of awakening into a butterfly state and becoming a free butterfly is one of practice, not perfection. The free butterfly continues to grow and evolve. As humans we are in a process of constant evolution. When we dedicate our lives to being a butterfly we continue to expand, and open our body, mind, soul, and spirit. Just as the physical heart is always pumping, the spiritual heart is always evolving. Just as the free wings are always flying to new heights, the free butterfly continues to evolve and fly to undiscovered realms. The human butterfly state is our natural state. In *The Beauty of Wings* I use the term miracles. I have come to understand that our natural state is miraculous and miracles can occur everyday for all of us as we return home to our natural butterfly state.

Poetry by Alexandra

Wings Fluttering, Flying, and Soaring to New Heights

As I feel the intense heat of change, transformation, and growth
within my inner workings, the land reminds me of my greater
purpose and the greater whole. As I watch the summer flowers
wither away and the birds flying south, I am reminded of my
own rhythms and I start to remember why I am here.

As I let go of strings, cords, and heavy rocks, I expand my
wings even more and start to feel the ground beneath my feet,
the air against my cheek and the heat of the sun. As I allow
my inner spark to warm my body with radiant light, I shed
what is no longer needed and I step clearly into my light.

As I watch the colors, the varieties, and the textures that encompass the
planet, I am reminded of the beauty of the whole. The strength of the
trees reminds me of my courage, the flow of the river reminds me of my
grace, and the sounds of the birds remind me of my own sensitivity.

As I begin to trust the process, flow with grace, and accept
what is, my heart-space begins to open like a beautiful pink
rose. As I begin to align with my truth, listen deeply, see
others with eyes of compassion, and speak with courage, my
wings start to sparkle and my body begins to feel free.

As I review the past, embrace the present, and look forward to the future, possibilities seem limitless. Dreams, fantasies, and mountain views seem too real to be true. The belief that I am free, the trust that I know myself, and the wisdom to allow my heart-space to guide gives me the strength to continue on the journey.

As I open like the radiant sunlight, dwell in my eternal light, and practice the power of love, I begin to expand my horizons and I can truly breathe. As I unconditionally love all that is, I am reminded of what is real and that only love truly exists.

As I accept my challenges as stepping stones, as I see my setbacks as opportunities for greater expansion and embrace my weaknesses, my heart-space begins to glow like the silver wings of an angel.

As I greet my fuzzy friends with open arms and feel the bricks of lead fall away, I begin to span my wings. As I listen to the purr of the kitties and watch the wonder of the horses, I begin the process of learning to fly.

As I forgive myself, learn to love my shortcomings, and speak from my heart, I am reminded of the connection between the river, the roses, the butterflies, the eagles, and all living things.

As I allow my wounds to heal, step into my radiant light, feel my own expansion, and dance to my own drum beat, I see the light in all others as clearly as I see my own.

As I remember the joy of running, the beauty of muscles, and the strength within my heartbeat, I eagerly await the moment of dirt in my face, trails beneath my running shoes, and wind across my cheeks.

As I align myself more clearly than ever before
with my heart-space, live with humility,
grace, and compassion, I am reminded of my own eternal freedom,
my true heart-space, and I begin to believe that each living creature is
only a heartbeat away from flying
FREE.

Resources for Healing and Awakening

Channeled healings and readings:

Dr. Katherine: askguidance.com

Transformational body work:

Linda Cotrufello: healthytransformation.com

Guidance for soul connection, self-love, and self-care:

Dena Carter: denacarter.com

Channeled spiritual guidance:

Sanya Roman: orindaben.com

Wisdom from Laarkmaa:

Pia Smith Orleane
and Cullen Baird Smith: laarkmaa.com

Energy healing, massage, and spiritual guidance:

Catie Sanburg: sacredtouchwellness.com

Classes for psychic development and spiritual guidance:

Echo Bodine:	echobodine.com

LaHo-Chi energy healing, music, sacred tantric dance, and retreats:

Beloved Heartsong:	openyourhearts.com

Yoga classes, spiritual guidance:

Louise Lavergne:	louiselavergne.com
Tara Cindy Sherman:	yogacentermpls.com

Eating disorder resources:

The Emily Program:	emilyprogram.com
National Eating Disorders Association:	nationaleatingdisorders.org

Books:

You Can Heal Your Life by Louise Hay

Loving Yourself to Great Health: Thoughts and Food-the Ultimate Diet by Louise Hay, Ahlea Khadro, and Heather Dane

Self-Nurture: Learning to Care for Yourself as Effectively as You Care for Everyone Else by Alice D. Domar and Henry Dreher

The Art of Extreme Self-Care: Transform Your Life One Month at a Time by Cheryl Richardson

Remembering Who We Are: Laarkmaa's Guidance on Healing the Human Condition by Pia Smith Orleane and Cullen Baird Smith

The Return of the Feminine by Dr. Rebecca (Pia) Orleane

Living with Joy: Keys To Personal Power and Spiritual Transformation by Sanya Roman

Hands That Heal by Echo Bodine

A Still, Small Voice: A Psychic's Guide to Awakening Intuition by Echo Bodine

Empowerment through Reiki: The Path to Personal and Global Transformation by Paula Horan

Reiki resources:

The Meta Institute:	metainstitute.com
The International Center for Reiki Training:	reiki.org

② Acknowledgements

I am deeply grateful for the treasures of light and healing I have encountered on my path of awakening including Dr. Katherine, Linda Cotrufello, Louise Hay, Tara Cindy Sherman, Catie Sanburg, Beloved Heartsong, Maureen Lopez, Pia Smith Orleane and Cullen Baird Smith, Sanya Roman, Louise Lavergne, The Emily Program, Louise Page, Windy Ridge Ranch, Menogyn, Monica Olson, Dena Carter, my grandma Julie, and my angels. I want to thank my mom for always showing up when I need her the most, and being a source of support throughout my writing and publishing process. I want to thank my dad for encouraging my creativity and writing, and my brother for writing me a very sincere letter when I was near death.

I want to thank Danielle Anderson, my editor, Sarah Hrudka, my photographer, Samantha Barger, and Balboa Press. This book is a true collaboration and it would not be in print without all these hearts and hands.

Printed in the United States
By Bookmasters